UNBOUND FEET

FINDING FREEDOM IN COMMUNIST CHINA

KIM ORENDOR

W. Brand Publishing

NASHVILLE, TENNESSEE

*Some names and places have been changed
to protect individuals in the story.*

j.brand@wbrandpub.com

W. Brand Publishing

www.wbrandpub.com

Cover design by JuLee Brand / designchik.net

Unbound Feet / Kim Orendor —1st ed.

Available in Paperback, Kindle, and eBook formats.

Paperback ISBN: 978-1-950385-50-8

eBook ISBN: 978-1-950385-51-5

Library of Congress Control Number: 2020949517

CONTENTS

Prologue vii

Chapter 1 Tripping Over My Tongue 1

Chapter 2 What's in a Name? 9

Chapter 3 What Doesn't Kill Me, May Leave Me Maimed 17

Chapter 4 And So, It Begins 27

Chapter 5 March This Way 41

Chapter 6 Gorilla, Man, Gun 49

Chapter 7 How Did I Get Here? 57

Chapter 8 American History: The Musical 69

Chapter 9 A Time to Dance 85

Chapter 10 Ballin' Like a Girl 93

Chapter 11 The Three-Self Church: Me, Myself, and I 119

Chapter 12 Martin Luther, the Pentecostal Movement, and the Holocaust 129

Chapter 13 Making Myself at Home 137

Chapter 14 Living Like a Rock Star 147

Chapter 15 Which Newspaper is Lying? 155

Chapter 16 Play. Pause. Repeat. 167

Chapter 17 Lesson for Teacher 175

Chapter 18 A Time to Mourn 183

Chapter 19 2008: Parents, Earthquakes, and Stinky Tofu 187

Chapter 20 Raising the Dead: Student Home Visit, Part II 217

Chapter 21 I Can't Quit This Place 231

Acknowledgements 245

About the Author.. 247

To my parents, Gerry and Nickie, for making life an adventure and encouraging me to follow my dreams— even when they took me halfway around the world.

"Come on, you can do it," he said, full of confidence.

I wasn't so sure. I don't really know how to dance—much less how to swing dance—and certainly not how to do an "around-the-world" move.

I watched him pick up another girl—one who was taller than me—and swing her around. She looked like she had fun, and he looked strong enough to do it.

But not with me.

"Come on. It's your turn."

I didn't want to hurt him. I thought I'd cause his back to snap and his legs to buckle. I shook my head, "No. I'll hurt you."

He smiled and stretched out his arms. "No, you won't. Come on."

For some reason, my feet started walking forward. My mind was screaming at them to stop, but they weren't listening.

I put my arms around his neck and locked my hands to secure myself. I didn't feel secure. *What was I thinking?* Getting this close to a guy...to dance! Dancing leads to hand holding and we know where that goes. I was scared, but he just kept smiling.

He definitely seemed to be enjoying the thought of tossing me around.

"Okay, kick your legs up, and I'll catch you," he said matter-of-factly.

"Are you sure?" I asked again. "I really don't want to hurt you."

"You're not going to hurt me," he said. His confident smile backed up his words.

So, I kicked, and he caught. I was securely tucked behind his back for my around-the-world journey.

He turned to face me. "You're not heavy." I would have married him right then if he had asked, but I was still too scared about being swung around to utter a sound. I'm pretty sure I just nodded and smiled dumbly.

"Here we go. One. Two. Three."

I was suddenly swinging from behind him, to the front and then back on the other side, where he caught me once more. My smile was bigger, and my fear was gone.

"Ready? One more time. One. Two. Three."

Once again, I was swinging and this time he caught me half way around. We were done.

Ta da!

"See? I told you that you could do it." I think my smile finally matched his.

Wow, I love dancing.

Will you dance with me?

The voice, more of a thought, slowly drifted through my mind. I looked to see who else wanted to swing me around. There was no one else there.

Come, dance with me.

I knew the voice now. My Father was calling me to come away with him and dance.

I can't. My worries are too big. There is too much to do. I can't.

Just let it go and jump. I'll catch you.

No. This is just too big. I'm too much trouble. Dance with someone who's more deserving, someone who's got rhythm.

I want to dance with you. You can't hurt me. . .unless you don't dance with me.

I pushed my cluttered thoughts aside and walked forward. *What was I thinking?* No one should be this close to the Father. My heart pounded, my arms instinctively reached up and wrapped around his neck.

Ready?

I wasn't ready. The fear of letting a friend swing me around the world was miniscule to putting my life in the hands of the Father. My heart said "leap," but my mind asked, "Are you crazy?" I just stared at my feet.

My child. . .

His soft call caused me to raise my head and gaze into brilliant peace that flooded my soul.

. . .dance with me.

I threw myself into his presence.

See. You're no trouble. Ready to dance? One. Two. Three.

My burdens swirled away as we spun through existence to elation. Fear was flung far away as I felt the comfort and strength of the arms of the Father.

All too soon my feet were back on the ground.

Suddenly, feeling again like a child, I looked up, smiled and cried, "Again!"

Oh, how I love to dance.

CHAPTER 1

TRIPPING OVER MY TONGUE

Halfway across the Pacific Ocean and three miles above it, it starts to hit me that I'm moving to China for a year. Anxiety and eagerness make for an unsettling feeling in my stomach—which is exacerbated by the various smells that have assaulted me since the first meal.

I decide to walk the aisles and check on my fellow soon-to-be teachers. There are forty of us in various stages of nervous excitement. My travel mates are easy to spot amongst the sea of dark hair and olive skin. Forty mixed in with 250 gives me a glimpse into what my life is about to be as we become forty in a city of nearly one million.

Our collective represents nearly every region of the United States and covers a massive age range. There are a few who graduated from college three months before, while I already had a fifteen-year-long journalism career. While all of us found the program in different ways, it became obvious during our pre-flight training camp that all of us were there for a similar reason. Unlike what most people were thinking, not everyone in the group felt called to be a missionary—which is illegal in China—but we did feel a spiritual need to cross the Pacific.

Part of training included learning about China's laws, what you could and couldn't say to whom, and when. There was a section on civil rights and religious freedom. China has religious freedom, it's just very limited. The sessions were long and unintentionally created a sense of spy-versus-spy. My binder overflowed with paperwork addressing almost every possible way an American can get into trouble in a foreign country. This was intended to send us into China well-informed and wise, but instead there was general paranoia. Since I didn't plan on causing trouble and I was only allowed fifty pounds per suitcase, I tossed out a large amount of paperwork. A few of my co-teachers brought their paperwork with them and had sudden panic attacks midflight. They rambled through a list of disaster scenarios that would make any Jerry Bruckheimer movie pale in comparison. So great was one teacher's fear that he tore pages into small pieces and took turns flushing them down different toilets throughout the flight. If it's true planes emit lavatory waste in midair, my co-worker added to ocean pollution. If it's not true, some poor Chinese maintenance worker would have to clear a lot of paper from tubes.

As we crept closer to Beijing, I practiced all the Mandarin I picked up at our introductory camp. It took less than a minute: *nǐ hǎo* (hello), *nǐ hǎo ma* (how are you?), *xièxie* (thanks) and, for some odd reason, *shénme* (what). Maybe it would have been a good idea to pick up the Rosetta Stone recordings, but hey, the language classes at the university would be enough, right? As my stomach turns, I'm rethinking my lack of preparation.

I made my way to the back of the plane where there was extra space to stretch. The flight attendant asked me if I'd like a drink. Sadly, they did not have ginger ale, so 7-Up it was. I did not know how to say this in Mandarin, so I pointed. I took the iceless drink and used my best, "shea-uh, shea-uh." She cocked her head and gave me a half smile. I'm guessing that my "thanks" was a bit off.

While I didn't know much Chinese, I did know it was a tonal language. The idea that one word could have four different meanings depending upon tone was crazy to me.

First-tone words are pretty easy, they're like a monotone: *mā* (mother).

Second-tone words go up on the end, like a question: *má* (hemp).

Third-tone words—my nemesis—drop down and then go up, a vowel roller coaster: *mǎ* (horse).

Fourth-tone words are the easiest, they're like kung-fu chops, fast and sharp: *mà* (scold).

And with just a slip of the tongue you could call your mother a horse.

I practiced my four phrases again.

The captain made an announcement that was so garbled, I'm not even sure the natives on board understood what he said because no one moved. Eventually, the fasten seatbelt sign came on—thank goodness for international symbols.

From my aisle seat I strained to see out the window. I caught a glimpse of the mountains that surrounded Beijing and scanned the landscape for The Great Wall. I figured an object you can see from space should be easily seen from a descending Boeing 747. Turns out you can't really see it from space or the aisle seat.

As the ground grew closer, I caught glimpses of buildings, buildings that look very similar to those found in San Francisco, which we left twelve hours ago. I wondered where the real Chinese buildings were, the ones with sloped roofs and dragons on the eaves. I kept searching in vain for images from *The Last Emperor*. Clearly I was not prepared for the 2006 version of Beijing.

Aside from all of the strange writing on signs outside the window, the first indication that we were no longer in the United States happened seconds after the plane touched down. Nearly everyone got up to start opening the overhead bins and grabbing rice bags filled with clothes and trinkets from their trek to America.

My fellow Americans and I were agog—the fasten seat belt light was still on, for goodness sake. There was no reprimand from any flight attendant. People flooded the aisles and we remained locked in our rows. *Newbies*. Like cattle funneling through a chute, we eventually disembarked and were able to make it to customs.

The Chinese official who took my passport was very official. I did my best to smile like my picture and appear trustworthy. He stamped several sheets of paper and my book and handed it back. *"Shee shee."* He stared. *Dang it, still not the right "thanks."*

We were greeted by Jen—a female version of James Bond and MacGyver rolled into one—who had arranged transportation for us. After quick "hellos," she gave instructions for reaching the bus. It appeared there was a gauntlet to run outside.

"People will try to help you with your bags, just say '*bù yào.*' "
"Boo wow."
"*Bù yào*, fourth tone."
"Boo yow!"
"Good."

I must have sounded like a babbling idiot as I made my way toward the door, "Boo yow?" "Boo yow!" "Yow!!"

All language skills were lost as the first blast of Beijing air hit my lungs. It burned. It smelled. It excited.

I was distracted by sights and sounds and soon found myself surrounded by a pack of elderly Chinese men and women grabbing my luggage and shouting sounds that made no sense.

"No thanks, I got it. Thanks, I'm good." Good job, Kim, your English is impeccable. They continued to grab and pull.

"Boo yow!" They still pull. *Bù yào*! They stop and stare. *Ha, I did it*. But the pause is momentary as they start up again. Within a few minutes, Jen is at my side wielding perfect—in my ears—Mandarin. My luggage is surrendered to her and put on the bus with all the rest.

On the bus, my view of the city is unobstructed. I still have yet to see one dragon on a building, but I have already seen more vehicles per lane than any part of rush hour in Los Angeles. California traffic jams may be bumper-to-bumper six lanes wide, but Beijing traffic jams are bumper-to-bumper-to-fender-to-fender as traffic surges forward eight to nine cars wide. (And traffic lanes mean nothing.)

I have a very sudden urge to pray.

Instead of heading straight to Henan Province to begin TESOL and language training, we are treated to three days in Beijing to see the sights: The Great Wall, Tiananmen Square, the Forbidden City, and the Summer Palace.

Our lodging is outside the city and, finally, I see a sloped roof and dragons. Somehow this settles it—I really am in China for the next year.

The full impact of my decision to move halfway around the world has yet to hit me. Right now, it feels like a surreal Spring break: Standing on The Great Wall where warriors stood hundreds of years ago, walking across Tiananmen where students were killed nearly two decades ago...it was a lot to take in, in seventy-two hours.

While meandering around the square and entrance to the Forbidden City—this is where the giant photo of Chairman Mao is located—I needed a bathroom and didn't want to go alone. This was mainly because I was a bit afraid of getting lost, but mostly it was because squatty potties were a major unknown that needed to be a shared experience.

The dreaded "squatty"—similar to a Western outhouse minus the toilet seat—can be as simple as a hole in the ground or as fancy as a sunken ceramic basin. The nice ones had stalls *with* doors and built-in, anti-slip flooring, while others were door-less and lacked adhesive strips.

Aside from making a person grateful for the Western toilet in their apartment, squatties could also lead to dehydration as people avoided liquids to prevent the need, as well as frequent buddy trips (friends make great doors), and well-toned thighs.

On this day in Beijing, we employed the buddy system as another teacher, Linda, was also in need of relief. Thankfully, being in a high tourist area, this restroom facility was one of the nicer ones. It had stalls, doors, adhesive, toilet paper, and incense. With most of the amenities of the West in place, I felt okay waiting for Linda outside and taking in the sights of my new home.

In addition to amazing architecture, Beijing is full of young street hawkers, selling just about anything you can think of. As I wait, two young girls come up and try to sell me various trinkets.

I run through my phrases: Hello, how are you, thanks, what, and no want.

Bù yào! They walk away with disappointed looks on their faces.

My friend emerges a few minutes later and the girls descend upon her. I tell her the magic password and she gives it a try.

Bù yǎo. Sounds right to me, but the girls stop, look at each other and giggle and ask her again.

Bù yǎo, she responds again. They exchange very curious glances and walk away, still glancing back and giggling every few steps.

Later when we're all back together, I retell the story and Jen asks Linda to tell her what she said.

Bù yǎo.

Jen gives her the same look as the girls. "That's not 'no want.' You're using the third tone." Jen types the word into her amazing phone with translating powers—I can't wait to get myself one. She starts to laugh.

"You said, 'No bite.' "

No wonder the little girls were so confused. They were trying to make a buck and some American is warning them against biting. We all had a good laugh over it and realized that there will be many more *faux pas* before the year—shoot, the day—is over.

But my vocabulary has increased: *nǐ hǎo* (hello), *nǐ hǎo ma* (how are you?), *xièxie* (thanks), *shénme* (what), *bù yào* (no want), *bù yǎo* (no bite). Not really conversation ready, but I'm getting there.

KIM ORENDOR

CHAPTER 2

WHAT'S IN A NAME?

After three days in the mega metropolis of Beijing, we hopped a plane to Zhengzhou, the capital of Henan Province, and the heart of the Peoples' Republic of China.

The Zhengzhou airport was much easier to navigate than Beijing International. There was no gauntlet of baggage wranglers. My luggage and I were safely tucked on board a giant yellow bus without a hassle or a single *bù yào*.

Being a major coal region, Henan seemed wrapped in a constant haze. It is strange and unnerving to be able to stare at the sun—a brightish orange orb—without sunglasses and not even feel the need to squint. I grew up just north of Los Angeles, when it was the poster child for pollution. Even on The City of Angels' worst day, it never came close to being as bad as this region in China.

The toll road is a massive expanse of asphalt. It's lined by tall, leafless trees. The skinny poplars are planted six rows deep, each row slightly off from the one in front of it to create the optical illusion of many more trees. At first I thought it was some sort of wind break like I had seen around farms in California's Central Valley, but then I remembered news reports mentioning how the

Chinese authorities are planting trees in Beijing and around the country to help fight pollution. The capital city needs to lower its pollution index numbers for the Olympics, slated to kick off two years from now.

During the forty-five-minute drive from the airport to Xinzheng, the home of Sias International University, I notice all the highway signs and billboards. The Chinese characters look more like art than words and the *pinyin*—writing using the Roman alphabet—is familiar but it doesn't make it understandable.

Thankfully numbers are numbers. Sadly, in China, distances and speed are measured in kilometers instead of miles. So noting the driver clocking seventy is not seventy-miles-per-hour but kilometers per hour, which is not nearly as fast.

After several miles, I learn my first Chinese characters on my own. There are small signs with a cactus-shape and box with legs (出口) by each exit. In days to come, I will see these same characters in stores and restaurants. I don't know how to say *chūkǒu* (exit) yet, but I will.

Allowing a few days to settle in, the university has arranged for language classes for us. I'd be more excited if they weren't so early in the morning. For the next four weeks, my early mornings are full of Chinese and my late morning and afternoons are filled with TESOL—Teachers of English to Speakers of Other Languages—classes. At the end of the day, my brain is so full, sentences tend to be a mixture of English, Spanish—picked up in high school—and very poor Mandarin.

It's not my new teachers' fault. As all of my teachers since first grade have noted, "Kim fails to live up to potential but is a delight to have in class."

Joining me in this pre-dawn purgatory are a Texas couple with nice Southern drawls, an East Coaster who pronounces aunt like "awnt" instead of "ant," a soft-spoken guy from Georgia, and a former teacher with an excitable voice.

Our Chinese teacher, Malinda, has decided that to make the full transformation, we need Chinese names as well. However, she wanted to get to know us first. In China, it's not uncommon for a newborn baby to go without a name for a while as parents wait for the baby's personality traits to emerge.

Until then, she tortured us with tones and more tones. After a few rounds, every word started to sound exactly alike. The differences were miniscule and try as I might, I couldn't hit the right note.

My most-honored teacher would patiently pronounce *zà, cà,* and *sà* and my most tired brain heard *shh, shh,* and *shh*. Certain days we all sounded like five-year-olds telling each other to hush up.

To avoid going crazy, I turned on the charm and snarky remarks to get through class. Thankfully, my classmates appreciated my humor, but they also seemed to enjoy my bungling.

Then, in one class I got a brilliant idea, a wonderfully brilliant idea. I realized I was trying so hard to remember what words were and pronounce them correctly that I was doing neither, so, I gave up trying to know what I was saying and just repeat it back. *Voilà,* problem solved, head of the class, well, at least no longer the dunce. (In hindsight, I should have concentrated on knowing what I was saying.)

Teacher Mal started handing out names. My friend Autumn was given two names: *Si Jia Yin,* which translates "Good News," and a more literal *Shao Chin,* "Little Autumn." She got two, and I didn't get one. Teacher said she needed to really think of a good one for me. This was not going to go well. I could tell.

Finally, the day came and I got my name, *Ji Min. For reals Teacher? A third-tone name? It's like you're mocking me!* And after weeks of spending time with me what was the trait my teacher decided best suited me for a name: Smart. But not like Harvard, like clever, like smartass. My offense was short-lived as I realized she'd totally nailed me. And I'm pretty sure "Fails to Reach Potential" was far too complex for me to learn.

Now that we all had names we could barely pronounce and never hope to draw correctly, it was time to get down to learning something other than *sssss, sshhh,* and *zzzz.*

If textbooks teaching English are designed the same way as textbooks to teach Mandarin, I'm amazed anyone gets it right. I wanted to be able to get basic information: How much is this? Is it spicy? Where's the bus to Xinzheng? Have you seen other foreigners who look lost?

No, our text book starts off with conversations such as:

"Do you want a cigarette?"

"No, I do not smoke."

"Oh, but you are American. All Americans smoke."

"Yes, I am American, but I do not smoke."

While this conversation would be accurate, I was pretty sure I could get away with the shaking head and finger wag to signal, "No thanks, I don't want that."

On the plus side, I now knew how to say, *Wǒ shì Měiguórén* (I am American). We spent the day learning the names for countries—America (*Měiguó*), China (*Zhōngguó*), Canada (*Jiānádà*), Mexico (*Mòxīgē*), Japan (*Rìběn*), England (*Yīngguó*), Italy (*Yìdàlì*)—and then practiced saying, *Wǒ shì Měiguórén; Wǒ bù shì Jiānádàrén.* (I am American. I am not Canadian.)

This was also the first time I remember thinking some of the language is just made up. Several words in Mandarin sound similar to their English equivalents, but in a silly way, like when Americans think adding an "o" to the end of a word makes it Spanish or an "i" makes it Italian.

Jiānádà sounds like "jau-nada," just as if Canada started with a "j." Or *Yìdàlì*, a shocking sounding, E-da-lee. Other words I learned that sounded super close to English were "coffee," "cola," and "lemon." Remember, it's all about the tones.

One day, I felt I was on a language breakthrough. *Měiguó* is made up of two characters (美国) which translate to "beautiful," and "country." So, I figured you could just say something was *měi* (beautiful) and call it good. Only I was quick to learn that pretty is *měiméi* and little sister is *mèimei*. Breakthrough evolving to breakdown.

Perhaps, I needed to hit the books again.

The lessons finally started teaching me phrases I could use. How much is that (*duōshao qián*)? That's too much (*tài guìle*). What is this (*zhè shì shénme*)? Where (*nǎlǐ*)? Do you have (*yǒu méiyǒu*)? Armed with these and my ever-growing vocabulary of nouns— apple (*píngguǒ*), watermelon (*xīguā*), noodles (*miàn*), eggplant (*qiézi*), chicken (*jīròu*), and beef (*niúròu*) —I decided it was time to take my act on the road. Finding courage in numbers, I asked a fellow California native, Keiz, to join me for a trip downtown. Her Mandarin and adventure level both ranked higher than mine, so I felt good about hailing a cab and setting off.

We had heard that there was an amazing noodle restaurant tucked away in an alley somewhere downtown. Armed with those shady directions, it's amazing we found the downtown on our own. As the only light-haired, light-eyed people wearing shorts and T-shirts anywhere in the public square, we did not have to wonder if the locals were talking about us. They pointed directly at us and said *lǎowài*, (which loosely translates as "old foreigner") and then giggle. At least they weren't calling us white devils.

Xinzheng's public square, *Yán Huáng Guǎng Chǎng*, was dubbed "Two-Head Park" by the foreign faculty because it's easier to say and also it was home to giant busts of Huangdi and Yandi. The historical duo watch over visitors atop a robust pedestal in the square. Huangdi is "The Man" in China, and according to legend, he's pretty much responsible for everything. It is said he invented writing, calendars, clothing, farming, and whatever was necessary for life to kick off in The Middle Kingdom.

I'm not sure what the locals thought about Huangdi, but they sure loved to hang out in the square. Various musicians would gather with their traditional instruments, some looking as old as China itself, and have pick-up jam sessions. Others set up tables to play Chinese poker—so not Texas Hold 'Em—or mahjong. The slapping of cards and shuffling of tiles gave the musicians a run for their money.

The square took up an entire city block. It was surrounded by buildings that housed some of the more expensive shops in the area. Most of the restaurants were located in alleys or on one of the many streets that led from the square.

When it became clear that we didn't really know our way around the hundreds of shops in the many alleys, we decided we should ask the locals if they knew where the amazing noodle restaurant was. We approached the first people we saw who didn't giggle and run away from us.

"*Nǐhǎo.*"

"*Nǐhǎo,*" they returned with added giggles.

"*Miàn nǎlǐ.*" (In hindsight learning proper syntax and grammar may have been helpful, because "Noodles where," is not really a solid sentence.)

More giggling and pointing to just about every place. Yeah, asking, "Where are there noodles?" in the downtown of a bustling Chinese city is pretty much the epitome of a blonde moment. At least I had someone to share it with.

We tried being more specific.

"*Hěn hǎo miàn nǎlǐ.*" (Very good noodles where.)

More giggling and more pointing. We thanked them and walked away to regroup. While we were no closer to the amazing noodles, we had learned there were numerous places to find very good noodles. Undaunted and uplifted by each other, we sought out more council. Keiz spied a pair of high school-aged girls. Chinese students start taking English classes at a young age, and we hoped their poor English and our poor Chinese would net amazing noodles.

We started in with our poor Mandarin. The girls exchanged glances and started to look around the square. We were starting to get a sense of *déjà vu*. One more shot. One more fail. Just when we figured we were going to settle for the closest noodle shop, one of the young girls spoke up.

"Do you know the name of the restaurant?" she asked in perfect English.

It was our turn to stare. She explained her father was an English teacher at a nearby school. I'd never been so happy to hear English in my life. We carried on our conversation in English. The girls, who already picked out a lunch spot, decided to skip their plans and join us, which turned out to be a great experience.

We followed close behind as they crossed the square and started down an alley. The type of alley movies teach people to avoid. The kind where crumpled papers tumble around and building siding is missing. But by this time we were too hungry to care. The girls stopped and pointed to a nondescript door at the top of some stairs.

"Here it is," they said in near unison.

There was no signage that I could recognize, but there was a flow of people in and out and enticing smells. We followed the girls in and sat around an old table on wooden stools. Turns out we not only needed the girls to find the place but also to correctly order food. We made small talk while waiting for the noodles, which arrived in a very large bowl.

I had long ago mastered the use of chopsticks thanks to American Chinese food restaurants. Sadly, they had not prepared me for long, sloppy noodles in a soup. The ratio of noodles that ended up on my shirt or the table to those that reached my mouth was pretty staggering. It was messy, but oh so good.

After saying our goodbyes, it was time to head back to the university. This was always the easiest part of the trip. If a foreigner hailed a taxi anywhere away from the college, the taxi driver's first response was always *Xi-Ya-Si* (Sias). All I'd have to do was nod in agreement, and in ten minutes, I was home. Later, when I started taking trips to other places, it was difficult to convince cabbies that indeed I wanted to go somewhere other than Sias.

But after a day of tracking down the perfect bowl of noodles, home sounded good.

CHAPTER 3

WHAT DOESN'T KILL ME, MAY LEAVE ME MAIMED

There was one glorious week before the semester started that I didn't have Chinese lessons or TESOL classes. It was a chance to explore my new home without anything getting in my way—other than my lack of language skills.

Other teachers were already coming back to our apartment building with stories of adventures trekking through the various villages behind our university. If you asked a Sias student, they would tell you Xinzheng, with a population inching toward one million, was a village. And comparing it to the capital city Zhengzhou's nine million residents, I guess it was small. But for those of us raised in North America, this was no village.

However, about a mile from our Americanized university, there were actual sleepy villages. I listened as other teachers talked of dirt roads, wild animals, ancient homes, and endless fields. I wanted an adventure.

I double-checked directions with Katie, who bubbled with excitement. Her high enthusiasm level fueled my desire to go find a bicycle and be on my adventure. However, it also made getting directions tough.

"Yeah, just go out the back gate and the other back gate and then across the railroad tracks. Watch for a train. There shouldn't be a train but just be careful."

"We have two back gates?" I asked.

"Yeah, there's a guard at the second one," she said, adding quickly, "Did I say go right at the railroad tracks and then right up the little hill? You turn left to get over the tracks but it's right there. Then you follow the edge."

"What? Wait, we have a guard?" My brain could not process as fast as she talked. "And follow the edge of what? To the road?"

"The garden. It's right after the railroad tracks. Watch for trains," she reminded me again. "It's a great ride. Make sure you check your bike for brakes. They don't all have brakes. Well, they all have brakes, but they don't all have brakes that work."

"What? The bike brakes don't work?"

"Have fun," she said, bounding away.

I couldn't help smiling watching her set off on her next adventure, like a dog chasing a squirrel. Katie made life in China sunny on the greyest of days. She just didn't make it easy to remember directions.

There were bicycle rentals available it seemed like every hundred feet on the street in front of our university. Students used them to ride into town. Locals used them to run errands. Teachers used them to explore the road less traveled.

Early in the morning, there was a plethora of bikes. They were crammed into the vendor's space, sometimes tangling the handlebars or pedals. By mid- to late afternoon, options were limited, as early risers had taken off on the "better" bicycles.

The process for renting a bike was pretty simple. Students and locals would pick a bike, tell the owner the number on the frame, which they recorded in the log. Finally, the renter gave the owner their ID card as collateral. It was a little easier process for a foreign teacher: Pick a bike, record the number and go. It was one of several perks of being a *lǎowài*.

The bikes were circa 1970 Schwinn knockoffs. They had baskets on the handlebars. Some even had bells. Some bells worked. Remembering Katie's words of wisdom, I started checking brakes. I picked up the back end of a faded pink bike, gave the wheel a spin and applied the brake. The wheel spun freely. Not so much as even the hint of a squeak of rubber on metal. So... not that one.

My attention to detail attracted the owner lady's attention. I used my amazing vocabulary to explain myself. I demonstrated, again spinning the wheel, pulling the break and pointed to the still spinning wheel.

Zhège bùhǎo. (This no good.)

I picked up the next bike and did the same thing. The wheel stopped, not immediately but at least slowed.

Zhège hǎo. (This good.)

She used way more Mandarin words than I will ever know. She said them all with smiles and nods, so I took it as, "Oh, yes, I see what you are saying. This is bad and this is good." She wrote down the number of the semi-braking bike, and I was off.

I rode the bike back through the university toward the rear gate. It was a fairly smooth ride on the cobblestone streets, the basket rattled but stayed on, and the bell tinkled but held fast. I passed one gate and was now on the dirt lot behind the school. (Over the next five years, the land would be developed into classrooms, cafeterias, and dormitories. But for now, it was an off-road paradise.)

Following the tracks of tires in the soft earth, I was soon at the second gate, and there was a guard there. He gave me a bewildered look as if to say, "You do know this is the *back* gate and there's nothing out here but fields." I did what I always did in those situations, smiled and gave him my best, *Nǐhǎo, péngyou.*" (Hello, friend.) He shook his head and waved me through.

Outside the back gate was a single-lane dirt road, used mostly for trash trucks, judging from all the garbage spilled on the road. It ran parallel to the train tracks, which carried mostly coal cars. The trains ran several times a day and night. Their engines were throwbacks to the time of Pullman cars. Watching one pass was like stepping back in time, and oh boy, how they took their time.

There was a small river that ran along the east side of the university. The train trestle that spanned this water hazard was not the sturdiest to walk on, so I understood why conductors slowed down to a crawl to cross it. One day, I remembered putting a penny on a railroad track in America and wondered what a Chinese coin would look like squished. I saw the train was at least a football field's length away, so I put my *yī jiǎo*—similar to a nickel—on the track and waited and waited and waited.

Finally the train arrived. I waved up at the conductor, who nodded in my direction without a smile. The engine rumbled over the coin, and surprisingly it stayed on the track. Three more cars rolled over the silver disk, slowly stretching and smashing it into an oval. It finally bounced off into the surrounding rocks. I toyed with the idea of going and getting it right then but had read too many stories about trains-versus-people accidents, so I waited even more. When I was sure the last car was safely by, I retrieved my flattened souvenir. The large number "1" on the coin was massively elongated, but you could still tell what it used to be. A student told me later I could get in serious trouble for that. Not sure if it's true, or just something his parents told him to keep him away from trains.

On the other side of the train tracks, the bike tire markings took a sharp turn down the bank. I could see them go up a berm on the other side. Taking Katie's words to heart, I double checked for a train, saw none, and proceeded across.

Once on the other side, I also understood what she meant about "the edge." The berm turned out to be a one-foot wide levee that hemmed in little lotus farm plots. The big leaves and flowers sat on top of the cloudy water, which was probably a foot or more deep. It wouldn't kill me if I fell in, but the water scared me. Who knew what was growing in it that would try to kill me over the course of my tenure? I stayed away from the water side.

It wasn't really any safer on the other side. The bank was about five feet high. Again, it wouldn't kill me if I fell, but it could do some damage. So I moseyed along the pseudo tight-rope on my semi-sound bicycle, hoping and praying nothing would cause me to need the brakes.

After what seemed like miles (but was more likely a hundred feet), the berm widened and dropped down to a real road. I couldn't remember the exact directions anymore, so I went with my gut and turned left. The road was full of potholes that rattled the basket and the bell, not to mention me. It was hard to find any smooth places. I was not the only one zig-zagging my way along this stretch. I encountered a few cars, whose drivers honked and let me know they were there. There is a lot of honking in China, but most of it is *not* out of rudeness. People honk as a way of saying, "Here I am. Please get out of the way." And the louder and more shrill the horn the bigger the vehicle. Bus trips were made nearly intolerable because the driver was constantly honking. Maybe a full eight-tenths of each mile was highlighted with the air horn.

Even with my limited knowledge of the country, I knew my anemic bike bell put me at the bottom of the food chain.

I was still looking for the village when I found a random store at an intersection. There were children running around outside, and a few bikes leaned against the wall. I took this as a sign that I was on the right road. People wouldn't want to travel all the way into town for supplies, and this was like an outpost.

The paved road turned into a hard-packed dirt road surrounded by fields of small green clover-like plants. There were smatterings of wildflowers. I was so enamored by the color and change in scenery that I forgot about the jarring potholes. Then I finally caught my first glimpse of an American-type housing development.

From a distance, it looked like the development contained maybe twenty-five homes. Their white walls and tile roofs probably had not changed in the last five hundred years. Each home was walled in with a front gate. Some gates were open, and I could look into the courtyard as I rode by them and see children playing, clothes drying, and women cooking food.

At this time of day, the only ones in the village were the very young and the very old. The rest were in town working or at school. For grandparents left home to watch grandchildren, having a *lǎowài* ride through the village was a sight to see. The kids would often chant, *Lǎowài, Lǎowài*, and run back inside.

Instead of children, I was greeted by a flock of geese. I had seen Canada geese in America, but these were giant white geese, whose heads were handle-bar height. They were nothing like human Canadians because these geese honked and chased after me. I wasn't really sure what damage a goose could do, but I didn't want to find out. I pedaled faster and ran into dogs lying by the road. Unlike the geese, they could not even be bothered to lift their heads to acknowledge me. I was so confused.

My antics caught the eyes of two grandmothers sitting outside their gates talking to one another. As I got closer to them, they smiled and pointed at something behind me. I assumed they too were talking about the lazy dogs and the aggressive geese. Their warm smiles made me pull my bike off the side of the road and chat with them.

"*Nǐmen hǎo, ma.*" I was so excited I remembered that "*men*" made "*nǐ*" go from you to all of you. I mean, why ask each individual how they are when you can cover them all with one phrase?

Their smiles grew and they didn't cover their mouths like most Chinese when they smile wide. My smile grew as I noticed their grins were missing some teeth. They smiled just as much with their eyes and couldn't quite get over me.

They looked at each other and had a conversation that I would hear numerous times in my five years overseas. (I'll keep it in English, but trust me, if I had to, I could write it in Chinese.)

"Ha, did you hear her? She said '*Nǐmen hǎo, ma.*'" said the lady, whose hair was pulled back tight in a bun. She wore the traditional blue clothing popular under Chairman Mao.

"Yes, I did hear her say, 'Nǐmen hǎo, ma.'" answered her friend, going with a less traditional brown coat and loose hair.

They went back and forth several times before stopping and looking at me again. Neither had answered the question, but seemed ready for me to talk again.

"*Wǒ shì Měiguórén.*"

And their conversation ensued again, substituting *Měiguórén* for *Nǐmen hǎo.*

I eventually exhausted all of my conversational Mandarin. I was getting ready to get back on my bike, when the lady in blue started talking very fast and pointing inside her gate. I shook my head, shrugged my shoulders and lifted my hands, palms up: The universal gesture for, "I don't know."

She tried again and now her friend was talking and pointing too. More shaking and shrugging. Finally, the lady in brown mimed picking up something off a plate and bringing it to her mouth.

"Hah, oh, I get it," I said in my best English. "Do I want to eat? No thanks."

Now they were shaking and shrugging.

While I was hungry, I wasn't sure that my American stomach was ready for real Chinese food and the bike ride out was rough on an empty stomach. No way I was chancing riding and being sick.

Bù yào, xièxie, I told them with a slight bow of respect.

And they launched into my ability to say, *Bù yào*. I took it as my cue to leave.

Their faces—especially those smiles—never left my memory. Their tan wrinkles told of countless hours working in their gardens. Their clothing style was solidly set in 1945. Before moving to China, I had very limited information on the nation's history. My elementary, high school, and college curriculum was mostly concerned with the relationship between the United States and the Soviet Union. Even after China reopened for trade, I don't recall hearing much. However, what I did hear was frightening and included stories of atrocities against people of faith, girls, and any opposition in general.

Once I knew I was heading to China, I started to study some on my own and I learned a lot more during teacher training in America. One of the cruelest things I learned was the practice of foot binding. Young girls' four smaller toes were broken and bound under her foot and her heel was pulled toward her toes, making a severe arch in an attempt to reach an ideal length of three inches. Small-footed women were considered beautiful in ancient China. My size-five feet may have paid off a century ago.

While the practice is mostly associated with wealthy women, it was also practiced in rural areas, before it was finally outlawed in 1912. The women I met in the village most likely escaped this treatment, but they surely suffered through the Cultural Revolution and other atrocities. My heart ached at the possibility that these beautiful women might have been subjected to any cruel injustice—to their feet or otherwise. I hoped they were becoming free from their crippling experience, just as I was.

I followed the road back on the bicycle. The dogs were still just lying there. It would be harder to find any lazier creature than a dog in China. The geese were gone, thank goodness.

As I meandered back, I felt pretty good about my solo adventure. I wish I knew more words but it was fun playing charades. I returned my bike and paid my *yuán* (about fifteen cents).

I patted the jankity old bike on its seat as I lined it back up in the vendor's area.

Zhège hěn hǎo, I said to the lady, who seemed happy to know the bike had gone from good to very good.

It was more the adventure than the bike, but it added just the right element of danger.

CHAPTER 4

AND SO, IT BEGINS

An unfamiliar ringing woke me from a deep sleep. I grabbed my cellphone, and fumbled with the buttons, but the ringing continued.

My groggy mind focused, and I realized the landline was ringing. At four o'clock in the morning. I pulled the phone from its cradle, expecting to hear bad news. Who calls at four o'clock in the morning if it's not with bad news?

"Hello," I mumbled.

"Hey, honey, just checking to see how your first day of teaching went." Mom's voice was way too chipper.

"It hasn't even started yet," I said way less chipper. "It won't start for another four hours."

"Oh, sorry. What time is it?"

"It's four o'clock in the morning. I'm going back to bed now. I'll call you later."

In all fairness, trying to calculate the time difference between China and California is not easy. China is fifteen or sixteen hours ahead of the West coast, depending on whether Daylight Saving Time is in effect. One of the first things I did for my parents when I was home for a visit during the holiday break was set up two clocks on their computer desktop: One with California time, the other with China time. They never woke me up early again.

Three hours later, my alarm went off. Despite the rude interruption to my REM sleep cycle, I felt pretty good. Before moving across the Pacific, I decided to start my new teaching job with a new wardrobe, especially since the university had a dress code. My previous occupation as a sports reporter allowed me to work most days in shorts and T-shirts. Now, I stared at a whole new me in the closet mirror door. I almost didn't recognize myself in the black-and-white flower print skirt, sleeveless white blouse, and cropped red jacket that hit me at the waist. I couldn't remember the last time I wore a skirt for work—weddings, funerals, and parties, sure, but not work.

Part of the charm of moving halfway around the world to work with perfect strangers is the chance to reinvent yourself. My new co-workers didn't know my penchant for pants, so when I wore a skirt or dress it was not a big deal. However, when I'd dress up around my long-time buddies in California, I'd hear, "Hey, you *do* have legs," or "You clean up nice." The former always confused me because my shorts covered less than my skirts did. Living and working in China allowed me to experiment with different clothing styles without the playful harassment. I still didn't wear skirts or dresses often, but they were in my wardrobe. I did fancy my jean skort, which provided me comfort and ease of movement while still meeting dress code requirements.

When I was shopping for "teacher" clothes, I specifically looked for red items. I heard it was the color of good luck in China, and I had a feeling I was going to need all the luck I could get. I had three basic teaching outfits—built mix-and-match style like Garanimals, the kids' line of matchable clothing that was popular in the 1970s—that I cycled through during the week. In addition to luck, I learned many students have a limited wardrobe and wear the same clothes all week. While I may in fact be a wealthy foreigner compared to my students, it didn't mean I needed to look the part.

I walked down a flight of stairs from my apartment to the first floor and joined my fellow teachers in the dining hall. While we had an American chef helping the Chinese staff in the kitchen, breakfast in China was hardly worth getting up early for. The morning buffet featured scrambled eggs, hard boiled eggs, overcooked fried eggs, raw to burnt bacon and two types of Chinese porridge. There was also fresh bread and peanut butter. I fixed a plate of eggs and toast and sat at one of the dozen or so giant round tables that filled the hall. The room echoed—literally—with the excitement of the new year. Its concrete walls bounced conversations all around and sometimes made it difficult to hear the person next to you. After bussing my plate, I rechecked my schedule to confirm my destination. I brushed off my skirt and headed across campus to teach my first "Readings in Western Newspapers and Magazines" class. Nerves—or breakfast—caused my stomach to do a somersault. The humid September weather gave way to a slight rain, which made the day less muggy but more wet. I missed wearing pants.

Per university instructions, I arrived at my classroom early so I could welcome my students at the door. (This practice lasted a few weeks. I was always there before the eight-o'clock bell, but rarely was I first.) A mixture of fear and excitement filled my heart and mind as forty-nine eager sophomores poured through the door. They were Business English majors, which meant two things: the class had high English skills and consisted mostly of girls. My Chinese Literature students were at the other end of the spectrum. They had very low English skills, and were evenly split on gender.

My first classroom had stark white walls with random posters of philosophical quotes from European, Asian, and American leaders plastered in the corners. There were even money-saving tips from "U.S. President Benjamin Franklin." I'm not sure how many people told the administration about the error, but the sign never came down. It made me skeptical of anything I read in China.

Adding to the Orwellian feel of the room were the bench desks. There were three columns of desks with ten rows in each. The outer rows could sit five students and the middle rows, eight. As the students filed in and filled row after row after row, I stood at the front of the class shuffling papers. Most students were talking to their classmates in Chinese, some glanced my way, and if we made eye contact I'd smile. I became overly aware of my hand movements, rapid breathing and shuffling feet. I wasn't afraid of talking in front of crowds, but I was very afraid of failure.

A conversation with my mom from earlier in the week came back to me.

"I'm so nervous," I confessed.

"Don't be nervous. They're probably more afraid of you than you are of them."

"Mom, they're not wild animals."

I chuckled at the memory and my breathing returned to normal.

The first day of class in China is pretty much like the first day of class anywhere: boring and filled with loads of paperwork.

My most-used teacher's aids were the student information index cards. This card was a gold mine of information. In addition to a student's Chinese name—in characters and *pinyin*—it had their English name, hometown, and section for additional notes. For my newspaper students, I asked them to write their news sources in the extra space. A few did, but most wrote how they were excited to become my friend. I was faced with the knowledge that either my students didn't read any news source or didn't understand the question. Neither scenario boded well for me.

As a foreigner teacher, I called my students by their English names. With five classes averaging fifty students each, the odds that I could remember—let alone pronounce—two hundred and fifty Chinese names were slim to none. That's still a lot of names to remember in English. Some of my students had traditional English names—Julian, Michael, Jack, Kevin, Sue, Shelly—while other names were more English words, parts of speech or surnames—Chocolate, As, O'Neal, Smile, McGrady, Cherry. NBA players were extremely popular sources for English names for guys and gals.

I collected and read through the cards to make sure I was pronouncing the names correctly, and more importantly, to begin putting faces with those names. True, all my students had dark hair and dark eyes. But that's about where the similarities ended. Sitting side by side, row after row their distinctive features came through. Physically, some had paler skin, wider noses, thinner lips, or protruding brows. Stylistically, they were even more all over the map. There were long, short, dyed and anime-inspired hairstyles. Clothing styles ran from the 1980s to the 2000s.

Since I was a bit slow at remembering names, it helped that Chinese students—like their American counterparts—are creatures of habit and sat in basically the same seats all semester long. By week three, I could tell if a student was missing. I didn't always know *which* student, but I knew one was absent.

I had five classes my first semester, a mix of newspaper reading and comprehensive reading. That first week, I passed out note cards five times, read names five times, explained class procedure five times, went over the syllabus five times, defined office hours five times, and gave a brief biography of myself five times.

In addition, the first week set the tone for the remainder of the semester. I was already starting to feel badly for the students in Monday's first class and Thursday's last class.

Monday's class was filled with forty-nine guinea pigs. I put the lesson together on Sunday, and Monday at eight o'clock was the first "live" performance. In my excitement, I'd talk way too fast and have to back track. Lesson points I thought were crystal clear drew blank stares, and I had to redefine terms on the fly. I adjusted for the ten o'clock class, which benefited greatly and their grades showed it.

By the time two o'clock on Thursday rolled around, I was tired of hearing myself talk about the same thing. The lesson was tight and on-point, having been refined all week, but I lacked vim and vigor. I did not receive—nor did I deserve—high teacher evaluation marks from these students. The following semester, I was saved from being labeled a total hardnose by this class when I taught them earlier in the week and they got to know the "real" me.

My easiest and best class that first semester met at eight o'clock on Tuesday. The comprehensive reading classroom assigned was located at 601 Building six. I was confused because the building had only five floors. Starting up the stairs, I was pulled along by the tide of students hurrying to other classes. There were fewer and fewer students each flight of stairs. When I reached the fifth floor, there was a trickle of students heading up a final set of stairs to the roof. The roof!

Once on top of the building, I came face-to-face with what would become both my favorite and most-hated classroom. It was designed somewhat like a greenhouse, and the room featured giant windows that provided plenty of light and cold and heat. Whatever was outside came inside.

I loved that classroom because it was a little oasis. During the class break, instead of putting up with large crowds and noise in the hallways below, I was able to step onto the roof and enjoy quiet moments with students. As the earth rotated and winter drew near, I stopped class a few times to have my students look at the sunrise colors changing in the sky.

I hated the classroom because it was six flights up. There were no elevators in any of the classroom buildings. The only elevator on campus at that time was in the sixth-floor administration building. Life didn't seem fair. When winter arrived, my rooftop oasis became a horrible, frozen wasteland. No insulation. My breath came out as little clouds, and my students—bundled in everything they owned—created a slight fog around the desks with their breath and body heat.

Mostly I loved this classroom because of the students it gave me. This group of sophomore Business English majors stole my heart and hold it to this day. I got to know them exceptionally well because I had them for three semesters. The comprehensive reading class was two semesters long, and the newspaper reading class lasted one semester. Most classes had me for one class or the other, this group was lucky—or cursed—to have me for both.

For four months that first semester, we walked up those six flights of stairs together. They shared personal stories during breaks. They invited themselves to my apartment to teach me how to make *jiǎozi*—dumplings—for dinner. I invited them to my apartment to teach me how to play *mahjong* for fun. They invited me to join them on bike rides and mountain hikes. Sitting in the stands and watching them walk for graduation three years later was one of the greatest and proudest moments of my life.

A group of students nicknamed themselves "Six Pack," and were among the first to take advantage of my office hours. My contract stipulated that I had to offer office hours to my students. It didn't seem to matter that I didn't have an office, so I was basically contractually obligated to have an open house once a week. As a single teacher, I was given a one-bedroom apartment, which was more like a studio.

My apartment was the first off the common area and one of the smaller units. The door off the hallway opened to my living room, which was crammed with school-authorized furniture. I was lucky that my faux leather couch had padded arm rests, unlike the wooden ones on the new furniture provided by housing. There were two matching chairs, along with a coffee table and two end tables. The couch and end table took up one wall, and I crammed the two chairs together to fit in the space on the side wall. There was just enough room to put the table in front of the couch and still walk unencumbered into the hallway. It was still just over far enough to cause a few bruises on my shins.

The narrow hallway doubled as a kitchen and pantry. The dorm-size refrigerator sat on a tile counter next to the sink. Off the hall was the bathroom, which featured a western toilet and shower stall with hard plastic floor liner. There was a trash bin for all paper waste. The water system did not allow for paper to be flushed. This was common all around China, and I adapted quickly. The hallway ended at the door to my bedroom with its white walls, old beige curtains, mirrored closet doors and built-in desk. The bed was a box spring sans mattress. The university provided a few comforters and a duvet. Instead of sleeping under them, I used them for cushion and slept under the bedding I brought from home.

I spent the majority of my time in the living room. I could sink into the overstuffed couch and put my feet up on the coffee table. I entertained friends and welcomed countless students for social visits and office hours.

While I could have as many foreigners in my place as I wanted, there is a national law that limits the number of Chinese individuals who may be at a home gathering at any one time to sixteen. To help with crowd control, I broke visiting time into chunks and had students sign up. Unfortunately for Johnny Law and me, some students liked to stay longer and others arrived early. If the crowd got out of hand, I'd move the "party" to the shared common area in the apartment building or outside if the weather was nice.

I imagined office hours to be just like what I experienced with my college professors.

Me: "Professor Smith, could you please clarify Point A in today's lecture and explain how it applies to my project?"

To which Professor Smith would give a brief, albeit, informational statement, and I'd be on my way.

But I was in for a surprise. That was not the China way. It may well have been the China way between Chinese teachers and students, but it was not the way between Chinese students and foreigners.

Some students were interested in knowing how to ensure a good grade, a few wanted some English speaking or grammar help, but most just wanted to talk about anything *but* reading.

That first week, I think I had the same get-to-know-you conversation five times. In each group of visiting students, there was always one student who asked ninety-nine percent of the questions, sixty percent of those were whispered to them from another student.

"You are from where?" asked the assigned leader, who took the spot in the middle of the couch.

"California."

"Oh, it is the most beautiful," she responded as the group nodded in unison.

"You've been there?" I ask, knowing the answer.

"No. But I have heard it is. You have brothers or sisters?"

"No. I am like most Chinese. I am an only child." This usually got a few giggles and approving nods.

"You are married." This was typically more of a statement than a question because according to Chinese culture a woman of my age should be married.

"No. I am single." The whispers grew in volume and a long conversation in Chinese erupted.

"Why are you not married?"

"I like the freedom of being single." Judging by their faces, this was not a good answer. When I made no attempt to qualify my answer, they decided to go in a different direction.

"How old are you?"

Before I could answer, one of the girls said that it is rude to ask an American woman how old she is. I acknowledged it was a touchy question, but I didn't care.

"Thirty-nine."

A mix of gasps and giggles filled my apartment. I imagined them revisiting the married question and wondering just what was wrong with me.

I turned the tables, "How old are you?"

The average age is twenty.

"Are you married?"

Giggles all round. "No."

"Why?"

More giggles. "Teacher, we are in college."

All of my students have been told they may call me Kim, but I hear teacher far more than my name.

"Do you want to see pictures of my family and home?"

A chorus of, "Yes" fills the room. I pull out my coffee-table book of California with amazing pictures highlighting several regions of the Golden State. In addition, I grab three small photo-albums with pictures of my friends, family, and my house in Sacramento. During my time in China, I added albums of my trips to ancient cities—including Xi'an, Beijing, Shanghai— because many of my students had not visited these places and were excited to see me there.

The California book was a blessing and a curse to me. It proved to be a hit with my students. They loved to look through it—especially the section on the Chinese influence—and occasionally would try to read the caption information. The hard part was the constant reminder it became of what I was missing: blue skies, cool surf, blue skies, snow-capped mountains, blue skies, Mexican food, and more blue skies.

One young girl sat staring at a picture. I couldn't see it because she had pulled her feet up onto the couch, her knees close to her chest, and was resting the book in a V-shape near her face. Her friend told her to turn the page. But she didn't, it was like she was in a trance.

"Is this real?" she asked.

"Yeah, they're all real pictures," I thought maybe she was confused by a photo from the gold country region that featured a cornucopia of clothing items strewn about.

"But it is so blue," she said as she turned the picture to face me. And indeed it was blue. It was an idyllic mountain scene, with jagged peaks, wispy clouds, and a lapis sky reflected in a mirror-like lake. I felt like crying. Not just because I was home-sick but because so many of my students had no idea what a clear sky looked like. During my five years in the Henan Province, it would be possible to cram all the clear, blue sky days into two months. The majority of the time the sky looked like a dusty slate. Some of my students went on to graduate school in the States—Florida, New York, Arizona—and the things that stood out to them the most were, the sky *really* was that blue and cars stop at intersections, "Even if there is not a stop sign."

The blue sky conversation was typically followed by a session on pretty beaches—which required work on the long "e" versus the short "i" sound—Hollywood, and then saying our goodbyes. The designated leader of the pack would look at their phone throughout the visit. I also was keeping track of time on my wall clock, not wanting to run long and have students stuck outside their dorms after curfew. Before I could say it was time to go, the leader would glance at their phone, stand up and announce, "Thank you. We must go now." The rest of the group stood up, said "thank you," and started out the door.

Thankfully, I gained my student's trust over the following days, weeks, months, and years, and we had real conversations. Occasionally, with new students, or when the conversations lagged, I'd grab the photo albums and picture book for talking points.

What never changed was the fascination with my marital status. Students either felt sorry for me, even though I told them I was quite happy, or they thought I was extremely brave to travel the world alone, even though I told them I had many friends.

With each passing year, I was able to reconnect with students before their graduation ceremony. Sometimes we'd get together and go out to lunch or dinner. We'd talk about our first days, weeks, and months together. I confessed how nervous I'd been and hoped I'd be a good teacher. They admitted they were nervous to have a foreign teacher and hoped they'd get good grades.

Together, through grace and honesty, we all made it through the highs and lows of the college experience. As they went off into the real world, I prepared for next year's classes, a little less afraid and much more prepared.

CHAPTER 5

MARCH THIS WAY

There are few things as scary and amazing as Chinese precision.

The Middle Kingdom was shuttered behind the Bamboo Curtain when I was a child, but photographs and videos of vast amounts of soldiers marching and tanks rolling around Tiananmen Square in front of the larger-than-life photo of Mao Zedong always seemed to make their way to my television. The annual October parade to celebrate the birth of communist China is part national pride and part international intimidation. It worked. I was awed.

Eventually, China chopped that curtain down and re-entered the world market. It was not a smooth or pretty transition. The information that trickled out of China was the stuff of nightmares—religious persecution, civil rights violations, government oppression—all of which exploded in the famed square in 1989. It was a scene that inspired—with its young people calling for democracy—and frightened—with an influx of crushing military might—all at the same time. The event was snuffed by a targeted government crackdown of the media and individual access to information.

Twenty years later, China charmed its way back onto the world stage. Like a rock star's comeback tour, China dazzled the world with eye-popping and jaw-dropping performances in the opening and closing ceremonies of the 2008 Summer Olympics in Beijing. Thousands of people performing in perfect unison. It was far less intimidating than the military maneuvers, but it delivered the same message: We are one.

There are few things that bond a group of people faster than suffering and surviving together. Military boot camps are designed to tear a group of individuals down to their cores and rebuild them as a mean, lean unified machine.

This unification is seen across all Chinese universities where incoming freshmen are required to go through military training. The length and intensity of the training varies between colleges. All of them are at least twenty days long, feature precision marching, and most will have weapons practice. At Sias International University, freshmen were subjected to three weeks of training, consisting of marching and standing. Lots and lots of standing.

Freshmen are the easiest students to spot their first month on campus with their deer-in-the-headlights stare and the camouflage uniforms. There are limited uniform sizes, which results in some rather unique styling choices. Many Chinese girls are thin, like an American size zero thin. Their uniform pants were typically bunched at the waist and their canvas belts wrapped around them nearly twice. Jackets hung off their shoulders and the sleeves covered their hands. There are also Chinese girls and boys at the other end of the spectrum, whose jackets didn't quite zip up and whose belts strained at their limits.

First-year students marched everywhere on campus in their class groups. And when they weren't marching they were standing. *Everywhere.* During my tenure, freshman classes averaged

5,000 students. For the sake of easy math, say there are fifty students in each class—English 1, Opera 1, English 2, Opera 2, etc.—that's one hundred units that need to find space to march and stand. At times, it was impossible to walk around the campus and not be surrounded by a sea of camouflage.

While the students at Sias didn't work with weapons, they were getting a true military experience. All of the instructors in charge of various classes were actual members of the Chinese military, and they took their jobs *very* seriously. I know from first-hand experience.

My first year, the school administration asked the foreign teachers if any would like to take part in a mini-military training. They explained we would be given uniforms—jackets, pants, and shoes—our own instructor, and march in the parade with all the freshmen at the end of training. They had me at uniform. How could I pass up a chance to get an authentic Chinese military uniform? I might not have been so quick to volunteer had I known the Chinese clothing size and fabric options.

The coarse green camouflage fabric made me long for my old fast-food joint polyester uniform. The pants fit my five-foot-tall frame like every other pair I've owned: snug up top and way too long on the bottom. On the flip side, I've gotten very good at rolling cuffs on pants. I had no complaints about the jacket, other than the fact that snaps seemed overkill paired with a zipper. The shoes were the worst part of the uniform. As much as I hate tight pants, I loathe shoes that lack any arch support or cushion in general. A thin piece of fabric separated my foot from the rubber sole of the green tennis shoe. I now understood why students bought homemade shoe inserts from street vendors.

Feeling like a nerd in my rolled-up pants, I channeled my inner high schooler to prepare for my first day of training. I drew from my extensive experience, which included two years in marching band and a year in color guard, but neither turned out to be useful.

Our drill instructor—the approximate equivalent of a U.S. staff sergeant—used a combination of translators and student demonstrations to teach us how to stand, salute, and march. This was not band camp. All of my previous marching experience had allowed for a straight relaxed hand or a closed fist. Now, I was required to have fingers bent at the first and second knuckle with the thumb down the side of the hand. I kept making a fist or leaving my hand straight, neither was acceptable.

The guys in my "unit" seemed to pick things up fast. The best was Mike. Our senior member, he also had the advantage of having been a First Lieutenant in the U.S. Air Force.

The drill instructor would call out for us to stand at attention. Head up. Chin out. Shoulders back. Chest out. Arms straight. Fingers straight. *Wrong!* He'd stop in front of me, an imposing figure in his uniform, and look at my hands. He shook his head and made his hand into the proper shape. I sighed at my failure, which threw off my shoulders and chest and arms. He called for attention, which I was able to pull off with satisfaction. Every part of me hurt, which is how I knew I was doing it right.

"You will stay this way for fifty minutes," he said with a thick accent.

"Fifteen?" I asked. I should have known that being at attention also meant don't ask questions. I received only a glance and then he walked away. "I really hope he said, 'Fifteen.'"

When what had to have been twenty minutes passed and we were still standing there, the horrible realization that he said, "Fifty," sunk in. (When I told my students about standing for fifty minutes, they laughed and told me sometimes they stayed that way for two to three hours.) My legs hurt, my back hurt, my feet hurt. I really wanted my over-cushioned, brand-name sneakers right then. Using my peripheral vision, I didn't see the instructor anywhere. I took the opportunity to shake out my hands and arms and wiggled my legs. Oh, what a glorious feeling. The guys were still at attention.

Upon the drill instructor's return, I did my best to stay at attention. He walked around us, inspecting our stances. He turned his back to us when another instructor came up, and I took the opportunity to relax. I was in mid-wiggle when he turned back around. There was no translation necessary for the slight shake of his head and finger waggle: Don't do that.

After a day of literally standing around, we got to the good stuff: marching. How hard could this be? I knew the Chinese words for right (yòu) and left (zuǒ), and I could walk a straight line. Our drill instructor brought over a small group of students to demonstrate the various marching styles we would learn and perform during the parade. He called them to attention. They hopped-to in perfect unison. He called for them to march. They started a typical left-right-left march. He called something that I didn't understand and they sped up. *Okay, so far, I can totally do this.* He called out another order I didn't comprehend and the group began a high-kicking, goose-step march. You could feel the change of attitude among the foreign teachers. I had seen other military units march this way on TV and in the movies, and none of them were ones I wanted to join. It was time for me to shake my head and waggle my finger. No disrespect, Dear Honorable Drill Instructor, but Americans don't goose step. And we didn't.

Once we established that we'd do the standard marching, it was time to form ranks and get to stepping. The left-right-left action was a welcome relief after all the standing. The difficulty came in the "about face" and "at ease." The about face was not the standard "pivot on your right toe and spin," there were half-steps and rotations and heels. Thankfully, after much head shaking and finger wagging, I got there.

At ease was actually worse than attention. At least at attention, I knew I was supposed to be in pain. At ease gives the impression there would be some, well, ease. Shoot, even the U.S. Marines appear to take it easy in this rest formation. I assumed that at ease meant I could stand with feet shoulder-width apart and hands behind my back. No. The instructor had a student demonstrate. He called "attention" and the student was ramrod straight, and his hands were perfect. *Show off.* The instructor then called "at ease," and the student moved his right foot to a forty-five degree angle. That was it. *Seriously.* No wonder the drill instructor was so intense, there was never any ease anywhere in this army.

A few days later, we were looking like a well-oiled machine. We stayed in our ranks, turned on dimes, and stopped in unison. During a break—a real break where we could stand or sit and talk and move our hands—the drill instructor came up to Mike and started talking through an interpreter. The young enlisted man had heard that Mike was a former member of the U.S. military and was curious about his service. Mike informed him that he had been a pilot for the Air Force and achieved the rank of First Lieutenant. Our tough-as-nails instructor went ashen as he realized that he'd been barking orders at an officer. Through the interpreter, he told Mike he wanted to show him proper respect and offer an apology. There on the steps of the administration building—designed to look like a Washington, D.C. monument—the young Chinese instructor in full uniform snapped to attention and saluted Mike, a U.S. veteran in Chinese camouflage. Mike returned the salute. He also assured our instructor that he didn't mind being ordered around and that he respected all men and women who served their countries.

The drill instructor had no problem yelling at the rest of us, but he didn't seem to be as loud as before. I'm not sure if it's because he was being nicer, or I just saw him differently now. We continued to drill and march until he was satisfied that we had it down, or at least would not cause him to lose face in front of the other instructors. On parade day, we marched around the track. It was easy to tell us apart from the freshman classes. Aside from our light hair and eyes, we were the smallest unit and the only one that didn't high-step in front of the grand stand.

While other Chinese universities end their freshman training with the parade, Sias goes one step further with a candle lighting ceremony. One of the first things I learned when I moved to China is that it loves its pomp and circumstance. If there is a way to make something into a grand gala, the Chinese will find a way. The freshman ceremony includes several dance numbers, speeches, and songs. It drones on and on and makes the Academy Awards show look short and dull. It concludes with the candle lighting ceremony. As the lights are turned out in the stadium, the first candles are lit and individuals turn to light the candle next to them. The glow grows on the infield grass of the stadium and spreads to the stands. It is a grand display wrapped in a quiet sweetness.

For the freshmen, it marks the end of their military training and the beginning of their academic year. They came to Sias as individual lights that were lost in the chaos, but now they are part of something bigger, something amazing. The bonds they forged during the three weeks of training will carry them for the next four years. The various classes started out with fifty strangers, and now they are good friends. When times get tough, they will use these memories to encourage each other: "Do you remember when we stood for hours in the rain? We can do this too."

For the foreign teachers, it was the end of a torturous—and enlightening—experience. We few, we crazy few, who took on the task, turned out to be the first and last group to go through the training. No reason was given, but it wasn't offered in following years, and I wasn't going to ask why or volunteer to do it again. My back, feet, and hands would never forgive me. Of my official three-piece uniform, I gave the shoes to a student, the pants to a friend—who didn't need to roll them up—and I kept the jacket. I had a Chinese friend write my name in characters above the pocket, just like a real military uniform. It hangs in my closet. I keep it not because I need a light camouflage jacket to wear, but as evidence that I really trained with Chinese military personnel, that I learned how to stand still and march straight, and that I never want to do it again.

CHAPTER 6

GORILLA, MAN, GUN

The only thing more abundant than red tape in China is pomp and circumstance. Each visitor to Sias University enjoyed a banquet, featuring the finest cuisine and a full night of entertainment with performances from the university's opera, music, and dance students.

Visiting dignitaries weren't the only reason to party. As with American colleges, Sias had student clubs and departments. Throughout the semester, different groups hosted festivities in either the campus's outdoor Roman amphitheater or in the more formal opera building. The events ranged from a simple game night or talent show to full-blown opera performances with fog and bubble machines.

With so many events, there was a constant demand for hosts. Most formal events were emceed by the top theater students, who took the stage in bedazzled dresses and ruffled tuxedos. Run-of-the-mill events were hosted by class leaders, and sometimes foreign teachers. Because of this, I learned it's important to get all the facts when someone asks, "Hey are you busy? I could use some help."

I didn't heed my own advice when my buddy Jack asked me, "Hey, Kim O, are you busy tonight? Do you want to play a game with some students?"

Earlier in the semester, Jack and I got together to play a little ping pong with students. I knew of several teachers who played Western board games during office hours. It was not uncommon for male teachers to ask a female friend to join the party if it was an all-girl group. I figured I'd be spending an hour with a few girls and Jack, and that would be that.

"Sure, I'm in."

"Great," Jack said. "I'll meet you in the lobby after dinner, and we can walk to the Roman theater together."

"The Roman theater?" I asked, as other questions started to formulate in my brain. "Why are we going there?"

"For the game," he said as if it were the obvious answer. He explained that the Foreign Language Department was hosting a giant game night in the amphitheater and had requested foreign teachers to emcee it. My brain shifted from thinking I was playing cards with four or five girls to hosting a game for approximately 2,000 students. I felt weak and sick to my stomach.

"It'll be fun," Jack said.

"What are we playing?" I asked. The Roman amphitheater was built into a slight hill, with the sunken stage abutting one of the campus buildings. The stair-stepped seating area held about 2,500 people, and wasn't conducive to any game I could think of playing.

"Gorilla, Man, Gun."

"I don't know that game, Jack."

"What? Really?" he said, as if everyone in the world knew this game except for me.

Turns out I did know the game, *kind of.* It's a full-body game similar to rock-paper-scissors. In Gorilla, Man, Gun, pairs start back-to-back and on the count of three quickly turn around and strike one of the three poses: Gorilla (arms high overhead and making a scary face), Man (hands on hips like Superman), and Gun (either finger guns or using both hands to hold a large rifle). Gorilla beats Man, Man beats Gun (don't ask), Gun beats Gorilla.

Every game has a prize, and the winner of this game would win dinner with the foreign teachers in their dining hall. It was a two-part prize, because students normally were not allowed to eat in the teacher's dining hall, and the meal typically costs guests fifteen yuan—you could get dinner for three to five yuan at other restaurants on campus.

I confided my nervousness to Jack, who assured me there was nothing to be worried about, that there'd only be like, "1,000 kids." Jack was good at calming my nerves that way. Before we even arrived at the amphitheater I knew Jack was off on his estimation. The top row of the Roman theater, which was at the same elevation as the first floor of the teacher's apartment complex, was overflowing with students who spilled out of the theater area onto the grass.

Weaving our way through the throng of students to the bottom of the amphitheater, I stared back up at a wall of humanity. The freshmen were easy to spot in their camouflage uniforms. The buzzing echo told me how full the place was since I was blinded off-and-on by one of two spot lights sweeping the stage. Jack and I were joined by a few other foreign teachers on stage, and I felt my confidence rise. Part of the reason for moving to China was to push myself out of my comfort zone, and I was doing just that tonight.

Once the rules of the game were explained several times in very slow, simple English and Mandarin, my first night in the spotlight began. It pretty much consisted of me saying, *Yī. Èr. Sān. Zhuàn!* (One. Two. Three. Turn!) The hillside was so crowded and the lights so bright, we relied on the students to be honest about who won or lost in the early rounds. When those standing had been whittled down to about fifty students, I called for them to come down onto the stage with us. Applause and cheers erupted as the students made their way down the steps.

We paired them up, and once again: *Yī. Èr. Sān. Zhuàn!* With each elimination, the cheers grew louder. My nervousness long since gone, I was totally in the moment. There was something oddly comforting in the craziness. The students on stage were giving it their best, rising on their toes, lifting their arms high, and scrunching their faces into menacing gorilla expressions. Others had seen one too many action movies as they drew finger guns from their invisible holsters or pump-loaded their shotguns. Few went with "Man," and really who wanted to just stand there like Yul Brynner in *The King and I*.

The final pairing couldn't have been scripted better. A petite freshman girl in her oversized uniform versus a male upperclassman, who was average size for his class but looked like Goliath next to her. It made you root for her even more. A final *Yī. Èr. Sān. Zhuàn!*

They turned, and her Gun took down his Gorilla. My ears were ringing as the students roared their approval. She was so excited, looking for and waving at her friends in the audience. I explained—in English—what she had won as she stood smiling politely as a smattering of applause rose from the student body. Then in Mandarin, the interpreter said she'd won dinner with the foreign teachers in their dining hall and her face lit up like a Christmas tree as the crowd went crazy again.

Her name was Li, and this was her first time away from home. She arrived at Peter Hall—the foreign teacher's apartment building—right on time for Monday night dinner. Unfortunately, I'd just had a horrible day in the classroom—unorganized and rushed—I was hoping she'd forgotten. Selfishly, the last thing

I wanted to do at that moment was spend more time with a student. But she was there, and I put on my best smile for the evening.

I walked her to the front desk where students had to register that they were in the building. Her head was slightly bowed and every now and then she'd glance up or out of the corner of her eye. I thought she was extra nervous, but the more students I got to know I understood this was normal behavior. Eye contact was a rare thing until students felt more comfortable around foreigners.

I hadn't been to a student cafeteria, yet, so I wasn't sure what Li was used to eating for dinner. The teacher's dining hall dinner menu featured an Americanized entrée and a mix of side dishes from both cultures. The Chinese sides were typically cold, high in ginger and kind of bitter. It took me awhile to try them, and I rarely ate them. The Western sides were recognizable vegetables. As Li and I went down the line, she filled her plate with everything that wasn't on my plate.

We joined a group of teachers at one of the many giant round tables. There was a lazy Susan in the middle of the table that was handy for passing things to the person on the opposite side and for spinning things into oblivion. Li cast quick glances around the table, answered questions when asked and even worked up the nerve to ask a few of her own. For a freshman, her English was above average. When a joke was told, we—the Americans— laughed loud, while Li buried her quiet giggle behind her hand. I silently chastised myself for wishing she hadn't come. This time around the table was the highlight of my day.

As the evening came to a close, I walked Li to the main desk to sign out. I never found out what happened to all those ledgers they kept at the front desk, but I pictured some poor office worker scouring page after page to make sure times in and out were properly recorded. I didn't sign in or out as a foreign teacher, but part of me was certain officials had ways of knowing where I was most of the time. It's not paranoia if it's true.

Li thanked me for the zillionth time as we said goodbye in the foyer. I felt a pang in my gut to offer Li my email and room number. She wasn't my student. I wasn't obligated to see her ever again, but when the spirit says "do something," you do it.

She had started to walk away and I grabbed her shoulder. She jumped.

"Sorry, I didn't mean to scare you," I said, handing her a piece of paper. "I just wanted to give you my email and number. If you need anything, just let me know." If you need anything– *what was I thinking?*

Her head shot up and she made full eye contact and then threw herself into my arms. The impact threw me off my feet, but I recovered and kept us both upright. As she held me in a bear hug, I realized she was taller than me by four inches. She seemed smaller the night before on the stage with the upperclassman. She buried her face in my neck, and not being a natural hugger, I wasn't really sure what to do. I had a Grinch moment. I flashed on the picture of the Grinch's heart growing three sizes as he hears the residents of Whoville sing. My horrible day and hesitancy to hug melted away as I hugged Li back and told her it was all going to be okay.

"Oh, you are like my mother," she said as her eyes misted over.

I was touched and then a bit shocked at the realization that I was indeed old enough to be her mother. It sounds strange, but I forget how old I am sometimes. I *know* how old I am, but I don't think about, and many say I don't *act* like it, and when you live with twenty-somethings and teach sophomores, it's easy to forget you graduated from high school before most of them were even born. Li was staring me full-on, eye-to-eye, and smiling, hands at her side. She did visit a few times but grew in confidence and found other friends—probably closer to her own age.

It seemed crazy how fast her confidence came, but it made sense because my own confidence had grown exponentially since leaving the safety of America and coming to a different world. I was fortunate to have co-workers who helped me in the transition. I'm a huge proponent of divine appointments—very few things in life happen by chance or coincidence. I'd been in China less than two months and already asked God a gazillion times, "Really, why am I here?"

Part of the answer was Li. It is not hard for me to believe that my life was shuffled around so that I could be in a faux Roman amphitheater in the middle of China to meet a young girl who was away from home for the first time in her life, and provide a surrogate mother's hug and reassuring words. The encounter was as beneficial for me as it was for her. I saw bits of myself in Li. While I had traveled far from family before, I'd always been on the same continent as them. Now, I wasn't even on a continent that spoke my language. However, I had picked up some key phrases, learned how to navigate the streets, and was starting to feel at home.

CHAPTER 7

HOW DID I GET HERE?

A
t least once a day since moving to China, I wondered—
sometimes aloud—*why am I here?*

Sometimes the thought came while trying to explain
the First Amendment to students, who couldn't comprehend
why a government would allow the press to print negative stories in the first place. Sometimes it came at the end of the day at
the grocery store when I could no longer distinguish between *sì*
(four) and *shí* (ten) and would hand the checker *èrshí* (twenty) *yuán*
and hoped she gave me correct change. Sometimes it struck me
while watching one of four English-speaking television channels,
none of them *my* ESPN. (We had the Australian version of the
sports network, which featured a mix of Aussie Rules Football
and snooker.)

Annoying and petty questions aside, in my heart, I knew the
"why" was answered by the question, "*How* did I get here?" The
short and easy answer was God, but that's too short and too easy.
The longer and more difficult answer featured a contemporary
Christian band, an agonizing application process, and a fundraising miracle.

The first time I heard Caedmon's Call was at a Christian
music festival in the late 1990s. I enjoyed the folksy style, with

acoustic guitars and soul-searching lyrics. The band received sporadic play on Christian radio, which was even more sporadically played in my car. Which is why, in 2006 when my friends Emma and Joel told me about a Caedmon's Call concert coming to the University of California, Davis, I was intrigued. And then I promptly forgot all about it.

In all fairness, my brain wasn't in the best place to remember things. Slightly more than a year before, I left my job at *The Davis Enterprise*, where I worked in the sports department for ten years. Before that, I had worked as a sports correspondent for *The Sacramento Bee* for five years. I loved ninety-five percent of my time in the sports world. I was paid to watch sports and then write about it. It combined the two things I thoroughly enjoy. As an added bonus, the California climate allowed me to work most days in shorts and a T-shirt. However, when I became sports editor, that five percent of discontentment started to take up more real estate.

I became tired of editing people's work and constantly being indoors. I wanted to write my own stories, perhaps a novel—doesn't every writer? I wanted to be active and outdoors again. So, I quit. I started writing the next great American novel—well, at least a novel written by an American—and realized without a book deal this was not a way to pay the bills, so I found myself writing greeting cards and packing orders for African-American Expressions. I was making money and working on my novel, but I was still frustrated. The longing in my heart was growing and it was going to take more than just writing to fill it.

There was this nagging that I couldn't quite shake. I grew up in the church, so a nagging spirit wasn't all that new. It had kept me in check most of my life. The times I ignored it resulted in consequences I'd rather forget. But this nagging was different, it was more of a yearning. My heart, mind, and soul were in a constant state of Christmas Eve. They were saturated with anticipation of something awesome about to happen. The problem was, it was spring and Christmas was a long, long time to wait.

Several months after the call from Emma and Joel, my "little brother" David called and asked if I'd like to join him that night for a concert at UC Davis.

"Sounds like fun," I said. "Who is it?"

"Caedmon's Call," he replied.

"Cool. I like them," I said, while something stirred in my gut.

We arrived at the concert venue early and found great seats. While we were catching up with each other's lives, I saw Emma and Joel walk into the building. The lightbulb went on, my gut screamed, "Now, I remember!"

"Glad you made it," Joel said.

"Yeah, me too," I said embarrassed that I'd actually totally forgotten.

All of us talked for a bit and Joel reminded me that the group from China would give a presentation during intermission. *The group from China?* I'd totally forgotten that Joel had been in China for part of the summer. I was feeling like a horrible friend and couldn't wait for the lights to dim and the concert to start. The music whisked me away to my happy place. There is something about that old-school sound that calms my soul.

During intermission, people started moving around the stage and setting up additional viewing screens. At first there was sound and no picture. Then there was picture with no sound. It was kind of funny, except to Joel and his friends. Eventually, everything was in sync and the video played. I remember the people's smiles most. There was so much joy in their faces. The video switched from faces to screen shots with questions:

"Do you love adventure?"

Yes.

"Do you enjoy being around college-age students?"

Yes.

"Do you want to teach in China?"

No!

There were more words, more screens, more questions, but I didn't comprehend them. There were more interviews with past teachers. I didn't really hear them. I just kept seeing their smiles.

"Do you want to teach in China?"

No! I said, "No" already.

No disrespect to Caedmon's Call, but I have no idea what they played the second half. A battle had started between my head and heart, a chaotic cacophony of reasons for and against going to China. I stared at the green information card in my hand. **Fill out the information below to learn more about teaching in China:**

My heart said, *"Fill it out."* My head responded with, *"They're not looking for late-thirty-somethings for this job, look around, you're at a university, they want young people."* A compromise was reached when I concluded there was no harm in filling out the form, and I even specifically wrote on the card, "Hey, I know you're probably looking for young people, but just in case. . ." Both my head and heart nearly exploded for very different reasons when the company contacted me a few days later.

The first time I talked to Matt, part of me knew I was going to China. Thankfully, the rest of me had about five months to get used to the idea. The bigger challenge was telling my parents. Yes, I was an adult. Yes, I was no longer living under their roof. Yes, it was a free country. But change does not go well in our family, especially if that change is the moving of the adopted only child to the other side of the world. The dust was still settling from when I moved twenty minutes away from my parents' home. Now, I was about to be a twelve-hour plane trip away. Knowing this, I set up a meeting with Matt and peppered him with every question I could think of that my mom and dad would ask me about the program. I learned later that after our conversation, Matt was convinced I wouldn't go because I had so many questions.

Armed with answers, I set my parents down after dinner and told them my plans to move to China to teach. I thought I was clever.

"Hey guys, remember how I had to get a passport for that cruise to Mexico," I started off with a light tone.

They both nodded.

"Well, it would be a shame for that passport to just sit around. I've found a teaching organization—you know how people are always saying I should coach or teach?—well, I'm going to go teach in China."

"Over my dead body!" Mom took it about as well as I thought she would.

I think they would have had a calmer reaction to me dropping the F-bomb. They assaulted me with the questions I'd asked Matt, and I bobbed and weaved my way through the inquisition. There was a brief moment where I think they thought about trying to ground me, but then I played my trump card.

"If it's God's will, you can't stop it."

There was a stillness in the house. Not a peace, but not a war. I quit my job at the greeting card company and moved back into my parent's house. It seemed right to spend extra time with them before I headed overseas. It gave them a front-row seat to the process, and it helped calm their nerves.

With my parents tentatively on board, I contacted Matt and began the application process full bore. It was the most brutal set of interview sessions I've ever had. At first, I thought maybe he was trying to get even with me for the interrogation I'd put him through. However, when I met other teachers later they expressed the same thing: It had been the hardest interview ever.

Granted, I'd only interviewed for four or five jobs before this one, but those first handful basically boiled down to: Tell us what makes you special and how you'll help our company.

I was confused and thrown for a mental loop when Matt asked, "Tell me your worst failure." Followed by what's your biggest disappointment, largest regret, most heinous crime—with only slight hyperbole. I answered with stories that most people knew, and he just stared at me.

"No. Your *worst*."

The way he emphasized "worst" was creepy and convicting at the same time. It was like he could see inside me and hear my thoughts. I found myself sharing memories with him that no one had heard before, that no one aside from the parties involved knew. I talked about being beaten up and bullied in school, about feeling scared and alone, and how the fear turned to anger and hate and then *I* became the bully. I wanted to add how my life eventually changed, but Matt stopped me. I felt cheated. I wanted—no I needed—to share something happy, something good, something redeeming.

I left the office mentally, physically, and spiritually exhausted. I felt about three inches tall. There was no way to gauge how the interview was going from Matt's perspective. From my side, it was not going well. I wasn't sure if I wanted to go to China anymore if this was what my future held. But, while just about every part of me was focused on the negativity of the day, there was a sliver of hope. A stillness that told me to hang on.

My next session featured Matt *and* Paul. I pictured a tag-team smack down about to fall on me and cringed inside. After a recap of the list of atrocities I admitted to the day before, Paul switched gears and decided to let me in on a little secret.

"You're God's favorite," he said without a hint of sarcasm or irony or teasing. "And while you're in China, you're just going to get to know Him and let Him love on you. How does that sound?"

It sounded as if I'd wandered into a cult. Or at the very least, it sounded like a punchline to a joke that no one had told me. After the previous day's third-degree, I was so confused, I wasn't sure what to think. Clearly, if he had read Matt's report he'd know that not only could I not be God's favorite, but also I probably should be shunned for a bit to make amends.

However, I knew he knew because we'd just gone over it ten minutes ago. Before I could answer, he told me again that I was "God's favorite." If I had a dollar for every time he said that that day, I'd have a serious stack of bills. My foggy brain was trying to find some logic in the process, and he switched to talking about the story of the Prodigal Son. I caught bits and pieces as he talked. There was the younger brother, older brother, and the father. People focus on the youngest, but the story is actually about the father. He knows all things the youngest son does while he's away and he welcomes him back. He works to reconcile the siblings. He restores the youngest.

I cannot count the number of times I'd read or heard this story preached. Enough that my brain typically switched to autopilot: Young greedy guy runs off, parties too hard, finds his right mind, repents. I was in this mode again as Paul talked, but he added something that I hadn't heard or recognized in the story before.

"The father was looking for his son," he said. "He wasn't in the house or at work. He was looking. He saw him a long way off. He *saw* him and then he *ran* to him."

Emotions overwhelmed me. I sat there crying as that slight sliver of hope within me that begged for me to hold on exploded into limitless joy. I had spent the majority of my Sundays in church, asked Jesus into my heart—at least three times—graduated from a Christian high school and even took classes at the local bible college, but that moment was the first time I really knew who God the Father was. And I wanted to get to know him more and if that meant going to China, so be it.

Once I was officially in the program, I told family and friends of my plan. Ninety percent of them were excited for me and this new adventure, the others were wary of my destination and motive. No one had asked me my motive, which was—in all truth—extremely selfish. Everyone assumed they knew it.

What I said: "Hey, just wanted to let you know, I'm going to teach in China."

What Christians heard: "Hey, just wanted to let you know, I'm going to China to preach the gospel to the ends of the earth, in the name of Jesus."

What most people heard: "Hey, just wanted to let you know, I'm going to China to be a missionary."

What people annoyed by religion heard: "Hey, just wanted to let you know, I'm going to China to bash people over the head with my religion."

Granted, there was a major spiritual undertone to my going to China, but not what people were expecting. I'm not sure how many times I had to explain that I wasn't a missionary, that legally you can't be one in China, that I signed a contract stating basically that I wouldn't push my beliefs on people. (The contract is in Chinese so I don't know the exact phrasing, but that's the gist.) However, while I wasn't allowed to proselytize my students, I was free to answer any questions they asked me, and they asked many questions regarding Christianity and faith in general.

It was extra hard to shake the idea of being a missionary when I was fundraising for the program. Each participant was required to raise $3,000 in savings. This was kept for ourselves, none of it went to the organization. The directors, Paul and Matt, designed it to ensure we had money upon returning to the United States because we were not going to become millionaires teaching in Henan Province.

My friend Lynette, who was familiar with fundraising, helped me put together a dessert social. A chance for friends and family to gather and learn about the university where I'd be teaching and enjoy some sweet treats. While my parent's home is spacious, the RSVPs led me to ask family friends Steve and Debbie if we could use their home. The place was packed and I worked the room like a politician: Shaking hands, answering questions, taking checks, and looking for babies to kiss.

Exhausted and excited, my parents and I went through envelopes and pledge promise cards when we got back to the house. In one night, I surpassed my fundraising goal. Tears of joy fell as I was overwhelmed by the provision. In addition, it was the last piece of the puzzle for my parents to believe this was the right path for me. The financial windfall of a miracle also included a cash donation from someone who had earlier expressed concern over my motives. I was touched by their note that stated: "I don't know if I believe in what you're doing, but I believe in you." I cried some more.

Dealing with overwhelming emotions was more of a challenge than learning Chinese. If I didn't know myself better, I'd swear I'd become manic-depressive or bipolar. In studying the Father heart of God, I would experience joy unspeakable as I realized I really was his favorite. (Also knowing that *everyone* is his favorite and because he's an infinite God, it's really not a big deal for him.) When I got that, I truly got that he loved me beyond measure, that nothing I could do could make him love me more or less, an amazing sense of freedom came into my life. Then sadness set in when I'd ponder all the years I'd wasted trying to do good, trying to win his affection, trying to be worthy, and realized it was wasted effort.

Nothing against all the churches and denominations I'd been a part of in America, but one of the great things about being in China is they don't exist there. China has a recognized Christian church—the Three-Self Church—but there's not a Three-Self Baptist or Lutheran Three-Self or Church of our Lady of the Three-Self. I was free to drop all the labels and just be a favorite daughter and learn from the heart of my Father. I was able to make my faith my own—not my grandparents', not my parents', not my pastor's, but mine—an actual real connection of faith.

That connection was the reason I was in China. In America, I had amazing mentors and limitless access to theological books, but they only scratched the surface. While there were a few individuals and writings that went deeper, most of what I heard and read fit into a nice little package that I used to define God and faith. I believed in God, had seen him work in my life, but I hadn't thought about developing individual relationships with God the Father, Son, and Spirit. Maybe it's because I was raised in a conservative Baptist church with a dash of Dutch Reform in high school. I'd grown comfortable enough in Pentecostal churches to raise my hands and acknowledge the Spirit. But I had come to the same place in my faith as I did with my career: Is this all there is? In a way, I quit my church the way I quit my job. I still love them both, but I knew in order for me to grow, I had to leave them behind.

But just like emotional baggage, you can't just leave spiritual baggage behind either. It has a way of hanging on. Every foreign teacher at the university came with some sort of preconceived doctrine or notion. Even though forty of us had been through the same recruiting process stateside, once we got to China, familiar habits started to creep back into play. There was a strong group of individuals who wholeheartedly embraced being God's favorites and embarked on a journey to discover His heart and walk in freedom. There was also a strong group of individuals who wholeheartedly embraced their church's doctrines and were in no way going to stop doing that now. In addition, there was a strong group of individuals who had wholeheartedly disavowed any religion whatsoever and were annoyed by all parties.

The great thing about walking in freedom is the ability not to be burdened by how others perceive your actions. In America, that's all I thought about. If I say this, will I sound too churchy, not churchy enough? If I don't raise my hands during this song, will people think I've lost touch with God? It's exhausting. I was able to get away from that in China. If I wanted to sit, stand, dance or sing during a worship service, I did. If I didn't want to go, I didn't. As I got to know the Father's heart I knew he wasn't the angry old man in the big golden chair waiting to exact vengeance on me. He wasn't keeping track of my church attendance or giving out gold stars for memorizing verses. He was waiting and watching for me and ready to throw me one amazing party. I had been drawn halfway around the world to learn to discover the freedom to party with the Father.

CHAPTER 8

AMERICAN HISTORY: THE MUSICAL

L ife in China is sometimes ironic, and other times a paradox. It has some of the tightest rules governing religious freedom and yet, for me, it provided a space for great spiritual growth. Other times, I found freedom through doing things I was contractually obligated to do. Exhibit A: Culture Week.

For five years, October was the best and worst of times. The month culminated in Sias International University's self-proclaimed claim to fame: Culture Week. While most universities had some form of talent competition that highlighted local culture, Sias wanted to exploit—uh, highlight—its vast foreign faculty. The late autumn event was six full days of arts, crafts, music, drama, comedy, and fireworks. Four of those days were planned and performed by the foreign teachers, in addition to their regularly scheduled academic obligations.

Rumors of Culture Week started during teacher training before we ever left America. Returning staff talked about dance routines, lip-synch performances, and the amount of extra work. Once in China, the overall enormity of the event hit with the full force of a *gung-fu* blow to the ribs. In a contractually mandated staff meeting, the university's "request" for teacher involvement was expressed, and "volunteers" were sought for one of four nights: Asia (everything but China), Africa/Latin America (don't ask), Europe, and North America (which technically includes Mexico, but not in actuality). There were veiled threats of fines and fees and woes for nonparticipation. Being a first-year teacher and full of excitement, I gladly joined team North America. My joy and excitement lasted about five minutes into my first meeting with head writer Andrei—boy genius—and upper management.

"We'd like you to tell the story of America."

"In two hours," Andrei said.

"You can go a little longer if you need."

You think?

That was pretty much all the direction we were given. Apparently previous Culture Weeks had been high in entertainment and low on education. This year, the Powers that Be wanted to switch that up. It felt not only like a monumental task, but a *boringly* monumental task. I'm proud to be an American, but I didn't like the idea of writing about American history for two hours, much less having to sit and watch it.

Thankfully, in addition to Andrei's writing skills, we had Shannon, who was returning for her second year. The three of us made a great team. Andrei paced the floor, tossing a Koosh ball to help him think. I sprawled on the couch, tossing out ideas and bad puns. Shannon—the voice of reason—wrote everything down, editing out bad ideas and keeping the story at a second-language-learner level.

At first we fiddled with the idea of how to fit Canada into the mix, but then we tossed America's Cap aside and just focused on America. It seemed historically fitting. We broke U.S. history into The Founding, The Civil War, Westward Expansion, Depression-World War II, 1950s-'70s, and the '80s-present. While we worked on the words, other teachers were busy coming up with performance ideas.

In the early stages of planning, we had a basic idea of the story and possible entertainment segments to go along with it. The problem was with the occasional new directions that came down from on high. Every new edict sent Andrei and Shannon back to the writing board and me out to update teachers on new deadlines or scene changes. Thankfully, most took it well.

After one last tweak, we had our set entertainment lineup, which included a waltz, a line dance, a percussion dance, and boy bands. Lots and lots of boy bands. In addition to helping write and boss people around—tasks in my sports editor wheelhouse—I was stretching myself by joining the country line dance crew. It may be hard to believe but I was a way worse dancer than marcher. The one saving grace of the whole thing was that the group leader was also my friend, Heather. She took pity on me and my two left feet. Since we were neighbors, she'd come across the hall to my studio or I'd go to hers and we'd practice. Well, I'd practice and she'd just do. It looks so simple in the movies. Left, right, cross-over, back, hop, left, right, kick, turn. Repeat. Not that I was the worst in the group, but I was placed in the back line. I could live with that.

In fact, I liked the back line. It was like sitting in the back of the classroom. I could get away with just about anything, and no one was the wiser. Line dancing also seemed like a good way for me to actually re-start my dance career. Okay, re-start is an exaggeration. Before China, the number of times I had danced in public could be counted on one hand, with fingers to spare.

If this were a movie, now is the time when the edges would blur as the film flashbacked to my youth for viewers to understand the enormity of my anxiety at joining the line dance team. Like many little girls, I took ballet, tap, and jazz lessons. Unlike most little girls, I hated it. I didn't feel comfortable in my own skin, let alone a pink leotard. Some days I wore a black leotard, which was only slightly better. As long as I've been aware of my body, I have not been fond of shaking, *plié*-ing, or skip, ball, changing in it. I wasn't totally against activity. I loved running, bike riding, and performing. I just couldn't find any sort of happiness in dancing.

Thankfully religion provided me an out later in life. While living in Colorado, the Baptist church we attended had strict rules when it came to youths and mingling: Thou Shall Not. Not only was dancing a horrible sin—though it didn't make God's Top Ten—but they also nixed mixed swimming. At the time, I was also deathly afraid of pools, so I was totally cool with the whole thing. My conservative parents came off as flaming liberals next to this group of elders. In addition to allowing me to go to the eighth grade dance, my parents drove my date and me there. Imagine ushering us into the gymnasium of abomination. My first school dance, sadly, was not my last. It was possibly the most-awkward hour and a half of my life. My date, a very sweet boy who was as short as I was, seemed as excited as me to dance. We managed a few stiffly armed, distant, slow rocking dances— my hands on his shoulders, his hands on my waist. Always at arm's length.

A lot of the time was spent sitting and talking with friends. There were some students who enjoyed dancing and were good at it. Or they didn't care what people thought and were willing to make fools of themselves. Toward the end of the evening, it was time to crown the kings and queens. Yes, our school had two sets of royalty: one elected, one selected. I couldn't have cared less about either, and if I could have driven, I would have left long before this time. By eighth grade, the cool kids are well-known so the elected king and queen were no surprise: The most popular boy and girl. The selected was via a lottery of names pulled from a coffee tin. The administrator pulled a boy's name from the lottery can and it was the king's best friend. I figured the fix was in and expected the lottery king's girlfriend's name to be drawn from the girls' can. I scanned the crowd looking for her, wanting to see if she could pull off a surprised expression.

"The queen is Kimberly Orendor."

The look on her face was indeed shock, and I'm sure it mirrored my own. My name? Why had they called my name? I didn't even consider the possibility that my name was in the mix. The looks on the faces of the elected king and queen and "my" king showed there was trouble in the monarchy. My date and I exchanged shoulder shrugs as I headed to center court for the royal dance, which, of course, was to a slow song. The king and I exchanged pleasant smiles. He was having none of the straight-arm dance, and I found myself a tad too close for comfort. Our feet tripped over each other, my hands got sweaty and our faces were too close for conversation. After the song ended, I relinquished my title to his girlfriend and was happy to get back to my date.

The next year's freshman dance was a 180. I was dateless, but went because there was nothing else to do in a small Colorado town. My previous date had not only grown five inches taller but also had fallen for my nemesis, let's call her Nemy. Every ninth grade girl has one; I had three. In something out of a John Hughes' movie, I learned Nemy was only going out with my former boyfriend because she thought it would hurt me. I honestly didn't care. At that point in my life, boys were still more annoying than anything else, but I cared about him and wanted him to be happy. When I arrived at the dance, I found him sitting alone and very unhappy. Glancing around the gym, I couldn't see Nemy anywhere.

"She's in the bathroom," he said with a hint of frustration.

"She's been in there a long time," I said more as a statement to an unasked question.

He nodded. "Since we got here. We haven't danced at all."

As bad of a dancer as I was, at least he had smiled when we had danced last year. The thought of him being hurt because Nemy was trying to get back at me hit a major nerve. I strode to the girls bathroom and found her and two of her friends standing and talking. Their voices echoed off the tiled walls and floor.

"Why aren't you dancing with him?"

She looked at me and said something that I'm sure she thought was funny. However, by then I wasn't listening to the words coming out of her mouth. I was moving forward, propelled by an anger I didn't fully understand. I grabbed her shoulder and pushed her toward the wall. I planted my arms on either side of her shoulders so she couldn't go anywhere. She was normally four inches taller than me but rose up to about six inches since she was wearing heels. The quickness of my actions must have shocked her and her friends into stillness.

"You are going to go out there. You are going to dance with him. You are going to make him smile. Or we're going to come back in here and it's not going to end well for you."

It was pretty obvious that I'd seen one too many police dramas already in my young life. I pulled my arm back and allowed her an exit. She and her companions left the restroom in silence. After they left, I wasn't really sure what had just happened. I also hoped and prayed that she would dance with him, because I didn't know how to follow up on my threat. After a few beats, I made my way back to the gymnasium. It took my eyes a bit to adjust to the dim lighting but I spied them dancing near the free-throw line. He was smiling. I let out a sigh of relief and found some friends to talk to for the rest of the night.

When we moved back to California, I enrolled in a conservative Christian school: No dancing. Yeah, my prayers had been answered. My junior and senior years of high school were dance-drama free, almost. My senior year, our "banquet"—that's what Christians do instead of dance, we eat—was held at a very posh hotel. It was also the site of another school's prom that night. We had to pass the major prom blowout bash to get to our meal, which was served in a small room at the end a very long hallway off the main lobby entrance. I'm not sure what came over us that night. Maybe it was Senioritis. Maybe it was that the food was coming out super slow and in stages. Maybe it was the fact our school administrators denied us a Senior Ditch Day. Whatever the reason, we clandestinely worked out a plan to leave the room, go back down the hallway and crash that prom. Note: I had no desire to dance but I had a huge longing to misbehave. Once our small band of brothers and sisters were assembled, our mouth-piece did some sly talking and people were on the dancefloor. Not me, I was standing near the entrance watching the hallway for administrative types. We stayed long enough to feel a bit bad but more excited for breaking a rule.

That rebellious day was the closest I'd come to dancing—tapping toes and swaying at concerts not included—until I signed up to be part of the line dance in China. Just the thought of dancing caused palpitations and light-headedness. Why did I want to torture myself so? What could be gained by getting *this* far out of my comfort zone? I hoped and prayed the answers would come.

While I lacked confidence in dancing, I had other Culture Week tasks that allowed me to show off a bit. In addition to the two-hour long, star-spangled nighttime extravaganza, each day featured cultural events in the morning and afternoon. I volunteered to design surfboards to be displayed in the California exhibit in Italian Square. What should have been an easy process turned into a three-day ordeal. The plywood we purchased was brought to the teacher's apartment building. (The lobby and ground floor around our building were a major construction zone for several weeks.) I drew the outline, and a Chinese foreman said he would cut out the pieces. I waited. He left with the power tools. I asked the next day if I could cut them out, he said, *bù*, that he would do it. And he left, *again*, with the power tools. Being bored, but mostly annoyed, I grabbed a rusted saw that had been tossed to the side and start to cut away. A Chinese workman came running over and took the saw away. My Mandarin covered food, clothes and cute kids, not construction, so I tried to take the saw back and cut out the boards. Eventually, it clicked with him what I was trying to do. He said he could do it, picked up the plywood and walked away with it. I followed on his heels as he meandered through the student dorms, down a dirt path, behind the stadium seats and through a black iron gate. He walked into a two-story concrete building that housed various machines too old for The Smithsonian. He plopped the plywood sheets on a bench and fed them through a band saw that sounded like it wanted to fly off. I hid behind the door. In a matter of minutes, the boards were cut out. I told him I could carry them, which caused him to laugh—either at my poor Mandarin or the thought—and he grabbed the boards and carried them back, out through the gate, down the dusty road, and to the apartment building.

I found myself in my happy place painting an abstract sunset on one board and hibiscus flowers on the other. In addition, my dancing was improving. I was still in the back row, but I was missing fewer steps and feeling almost confident. That should have been a clue that things were about to change. That I was about to be shoved a little further away from my comfort zone.

The script had evolved into *Bill and Ted's Excellent Adventure* meets *Back to the Future* (with sincere apologizes to both films). Our story involved The Professor and his assistant Joey. The Professor had invented a time machine and wanted to try it out. The Professor and Joey would stop in different eras and see what life was like in America. Sounded great to me. In my head, Andrei was easily The Professor. He was the most experienced actor and he'd written it, so it would be faster for him. Shannon was committed to dancing in Europe night, and so was not up for Joey. I figured the next logical step was Keiz, whose energy seemed perfect. However, she felt better suited to be stage manager, so all eyes and the role of Joey came to me. I was excited, nervous and a tad annoyed all at the same time. Excited for the chance, nervous because I knew the amphitheater would be even more crowded than Gorilla, Gun, Man and annoyed because I'd spent all that time learning to line dance.

My annoyance turned to apprehension as I learned that not only would Joey still be part of the line dance but now the character would also be roped. Yes, *roped*. Fellow teacher and Texan, Sloan, had been working on finding a rope in China to show off his rope trick skills. He succeeded and somehow—I must have missed a meeting—it was decided that part of the trick would be roping Joey, who makes Bill and Ted look super smart. Perhaps worse than the roping, I was now in the front line. I had lost sight of my comfort zone.

Heather and all the line dancers were great sports as my switch to Joey forced yet another change to the dance they'd been working on for weeks. To minimize impact, it was decided that Joey would be "left unattended" and told to "stay put" as The Professor went off to explore The West. Once he left, music would play and the ranch hands would start dancing. Joey was to fight an inner battle of following orders and wanting to join the dance, eventually giving in to the music. The foreman, Sloan, would arrive and become angry at the lack of work and naturally rope the interloping outsider, Joey. Seemed easy enough.

I didn't like being in the front line of dancers but being in the front as Joey was different. As a character, especially a goofball, I wasn't supposed to be good. So the fact that I wasn't good worked to my advantage. Ironically, I now actually knew the dance. Practices were much easier with the pressure off to hit all the steps. Now my only trepidation was being roped. I had to behave as if I didn't know some guy was about to wrangle me up. That was harder than keeping an eight-count in my head.

Culture Week kicked off with China Day, which is put together by the school and turns the campus into a Western-style Chinatown. Vendors fill up Italian Square—a major intersection on campus that features shops on the first floor and dorm rooms on the upper floors. There were kite makers, paper cutters, stone carvers, scroll painters, dancers, drummers, and a martial arts demonstration. I had seen intricate, lacy paper cuttings done by lasers in various greeting card stores in America. Watching the Chinese artisans produce complex and delicate patterns by hand with clunky metal scissors was mind-blowing. One lady folded a red sheet of paper several times, made a few snips here and there, opened and re-folded, a few more snips, refold, snip, and then unfurled a cutout of two birds surrounded by flowers. *Magic.*

Day Two was Asia Day. I taught class most of this day, so I didn't see anything in the square. I did meander to the amphitheater to catch the evening's performances. It was nice to sit and watch friends and acquaintances perform dances from around the Pacific Rim. The following day featured Africa/

Latin America/Mexico. Some teachers found avocados in the market place and made a batch of guacamole and served it with homemade tortilla chips. The evening again featured loads of dancing. The highlight of the night was the *piñata* of near death. It is not a good idea to give a Chinese student a heavy wooden pole to swing when he really doesn't know what you're telling him to do. It was only one of numerous safety violations committed daily on our campus. OSHA operatives would go insane in China. So far, no one else seemed to have been given the "make it educational" memo.

Day Four was European Day. It was also my day off. However, my excitement at spending my day in the square was thwarted by my need to make last minute preparations for America Day. I was looking forward to taking in the evening's performances. Team Europe had come up with a great idea of starting the night in Italian Square with Carnival and then moving the show into the amphitheater. About an hour before show time, I was approached by Chris, Europe's team leader. He asked if I would be part of the pyrotechnic crew. While I was looking forward to relaxing in a front row seat, lighting professional-grade fireworks sounded like a fun evening. Chris added that he was hoping I could keep an eye on the rest of the pyro crew, which consisted of teenaged boys: Tommy, Stephen, and Brian. *Sure, what could go wrong?*

The pyro crew had two missions: Start the show with fireworks, and end the show with fireworks. Chris had placed six boxes, containing twenty rockets each, around the roof in Italian Square. Because of the high wall on the roof, it wasn't easy to see down into the square. Stephen perched on a ledge and watched for Chris' signal, then we would light one or two boxes. The signal came and five of the six boxes went off perfectly. The last one was several minutes behind, and I thought, *Chris is not going to like that.* Overshadowing the late fireworks were the lifeless doves that the team tried to release. From the roof, there was a brief glimpse of two white objects being tossed toward the sky, perhaps they flapped or fluttered, but they quickly fell out of the sky and into the crowd. I have no idea what happened next because now myself and three teens were running to take up our positions on the roof of the six-story building next to the amphitheater. (It was a good thing I'd been hiking six floors twice a week that semester.)

We scaled the stairs and scrambled out the glass building and onto the roof. This roof was crowded with satellite dishes and antennae. Instead of a little classroom, this roof was home to the school's transmission center. Tommy informed the man at the desk that there would be fireworks in about ten minutes and he may want to take his headphones off to avoid going deaf. As the show continued on the stage below us, the four of us were deciding the best place to put the fireworks to get the maximum effect. One boy wanted it on the ledge, but relented when we convinced him that if it fell off to the performance below, that would be bad. One boy wanted it angled slightly, but he was swayed by reason that "aiming" a box of fireworks toward a crowd was more an act of aggression than entertainment. One boy found a nice flat spot away from satellite dishes and antennae. And then we backed away and waited for the cue.

Riverdance was the finale. It lasted four minutes, twenty seconds. Chris told us wait four minutes and then light the fuse so the fireworks would go off with the end of the dance. Solid planning. However, Chris did not factor curiosity or Brian into his equation. While three of us were watching the dance from above—a literal bird's-eye view—Brian wanted to check on the box one more time. Aside from a faint glow from the workman's room, the roof was dark. A sound from behind made us turn around, all I could see was an outline of a person hunched over a box. Suddenly, there was a flash of light as a lighter was flicked.

"What are you doing? It's not time."

Brian's face was half-lit, half-shadowed as he turned towards us. "I'm looking for the fuse."

"You don't look for a fuse with a lighter," I said. Tommy and Stephan had flashlights in their possession.

"It's okay," he said, as he moved the lighter back and forth around the box. "I'm just trying to find the fu..."

And then we all heard the tell-tale *hssssss* of a fuse igniting. The dancers weren't even a minute into the dance. Bless his heart, he tried to put it out with his fingers. He even stomped on it a bit before I convinced him to get away from the box just in case. Tommy was running to tell the operator the fireworks were going early and to take off his headset. There was a long pause.

"Hey maybe I put it out," Brian said as he started back to the box. "Maybe they won't go off..."

And before he could finish, off they went. I thought of Chris and his precision planning, and I thought of Shannon dancing under a shower of falling ash. It was such a crazy set of circumstances that no one could really be a mad at the four of us. However, the formation of the next pyro team was more selective.

Friday was America Day. Okay, technically, North America Day, but we'd already lost Mexico to Latin America, so who were we really fooling? Happy America Day.

My morning was spent hauling surfboards to Italian Square and directing the pouring of dirt for a sandcastle building area. Due to obligations in the night performance, my daytime fun was cut short. Andrei and I were fitted with white lab coats—we borrowed from the on-campus medical clinic—and reviewed the evening's script one more time. I checked in with all the acts. Keiz had the props in order. We were ready to go.

The lights dimmed. The spotlights came up. Andrei and I were replaced by The Professor and Joey. The students went crazy. The Professor whipped them into a frenzy as he explained the plan to travel through time and the need for them to help power the time machine. It's powered by the phrase, "Time machine, go!" As their chants grew louder, fog machines kicked on and the machine was ready to launch. First stop: The Founding. Like Peabody and Mr. Sherman, we set up the scenes and let the actors and dancers do their stuff.

We jumped to the Civil War, which featured a traditional waltz to "Tara," the theme from *Gone With the Wind*. This simple dance to this well-known song set the mood, because it was hard to find a Chinese student who had not seen and loved the epic film. As soon as the first notes of the song filled the amphitheater the students were screaming and cheering louder.

Westward Expansion was next and my nervousness kicked up a notch. The Professor and I got the students to make the time machine go, and suddenly we were in the west. There were a group of cowboys loitering on one side of the stage.

"Joey, I'm going to look around," The Professor said. "You stay right here."

"Right here," I echoed, pointing at my feet.

"Don't get into trouble!"

"Don't get into trouble," I aped. "Stay right here."

He walked away and the music started. The cowboys moseyed over and formed lines. They started the dance. A dance I knew. A dance I really wanted to be a part of right then.

"Stay here," I said, as I started to tap my feet and mimic the dancers. Each time I scooted a bit closer, I could hear the students laughing and "ooing" as I disobeyed The Professor and left my spot.

Now, I was on the edge of the line, following along, not perfectly, but close enough. For a moment, I wasn't me, I wasn't Joey, I was just dancing. I was moving and I was comfortable with it and me.

"Gotcha!" Sloan said, as the rope slipped over my head and caught me short. My comfortable moment was over. "Whatcha'all doing? Everyone get back to work."

The cowpokes ran off and The Professor came back. In rehearsals, Andrei and Sloan talked a little bit about roping and life in the west. Sloan was then going to do some tricks and rope a sawhorse. However, Andrei decided it would be better if *I* was roped *again*. I have to admit it was a funny bit and the students enjoyed it. The emotional and rope burn scars eventually healed.

With my dance number behind me, the rest of the night was easy. We traveled to World War II and met Rosie the Riveter. This stomp-like percussion dance featured washboards, metal pipes, empty water bottles, paint cans, and tin cans. I had never seen anything like it, but it was apparently very popular on college campuses.

The night ended with a tribute to boy bands, including NSYNC and The Backstreet Boys. The guys, wearing perfect period clothing, did a great job of re-enacting the stereotypical dance moves as they lip-synced to the songs. The decibel level of student's screams was mind-numbing and ear-drum blowing. There is something very intoxicating about cheers. I had heard them as an athlete and it thrilled me. Now, it was more of an encouragement. I understood that my students were going to cheer long and loud for me, no matter how well or poorly I actually performed. They were too polite to boo or say bad things. There was no way I could fail on a stage in China, which opened the door to many more risk-taking adventures.

CHAPTER 9

A TIME TO DANCE

Despite my aversion to dancing, I talked a good game in high school about how great I thought it was and how much I enjoyed it. Pretending to like it made life interesting in a private school. Remember, the place with the no-dancing rule? And who knew I'd fake it until I actually made it?

I was a horrible dancer, but I was a brilliant button pusher. I purposefully took the opposite point of view during Bible class discussions just to annoy my classmates and teacher. Aiding me in my quest to find my teacher's tipping point was the release of the movie, *Footloose*. This film followed a big city boy as he moved to a backwoods town with a no-dancing policy, enforced by the town's staunch preacher. My friends and I saw the movie several times and listened to the soundtrack until the cassette tape—yes, I'm talking about the original *Footloose*—was almost frayed.

When it came time to pick the Bible verse for the senior page of the yearbook, we thought we'd try the ending of Ecclesiastes 3:4: "A time to dance." I'm not sure how much the movie influenced us, or if we just wanted to see how far we could push the administration. We learned it was not very flexible and our verse was rejected. Since our page couldn't be verse-less, we went with the next verse on our list, Isaiah 40:31: "But they that wait upon the LORD shall renew their strength; they shall mount up with wings as eagles; they shall run, and not be weary; and they shall walk, and not faint." But several of us signed our year books with "Ecc 3:4."

My college experience was pretty much like high school, but with a full-time job to boot. I went to classes, got okay grades, and avoided social events that required moving to a beat. Transitioning to a full-time sports reporting job after graduation, dance was even less of a topic of conversation. If it wasn't for weddings, it's possible I could have avoided dancing altogether.

After decades of bliss, China's incessant need for pageantry knocked this flower off the wall. The mandated performances were offset by impromptu, rooftop parties at the teacher's apartment building. It was a chance to blow off some steam and forget—even if just for a night—that we were so far from home. I used the first rooftop shindigs to keep my line dancing skills sharp. I even learned the Electric Slide. It still felt extremely odd trying to move my feet, arms, legs, torso, and head to a beat, but there was such a great energy at the party that it was hard to sit still. And my friends were even more gracious than my students in encouraging me. They were all thumbs up and smiles.

Feeling a bit cocky and adventurous, I tagged along with Keiz to a student dance party. She explained that a student of hers had arranged a rave-like party on the steps of the administration building. It was an exceptionally cold night, the kind where you can see your breath, and where your knees knock together involuntarily. We made our way toward the building and could hear the party before we saw it. Once we crested the road, it was a sight to see. Lights flashed a rainbow of colors on the dance floor—a cordoned off section of the square—and splashed onto the steps of the admin building. Not a big fan of techno music, I was tempted to turn around, but I didn't want to lose face. Plus, it was too cold to walk all the way back to the apartment building.

We made our way to the bustling crowd and were mobbed by students, who were excited to see foreigners at their party. At first—like always—the students were so distracted by our presence they forgot what they were doing and just stared at us. Thankfully, as Keiz started to dance and I attempted to bob and weave to the beat of the music, the students remembered they were supposed to be dancing too. With fewer eyes on me, I was free to attempt to be free on the dance floor. The hard part was that my dance steps were very limited and techno and country line dancing really don't meld. I just copied Keiz.

As the night wore on, I started to fade and slowly eased my way toward the outer edge of the pack. This helped my hearing and gave me some room to move, but it also resulted in a sudden drop in body temperature. While dancing in the center was tiring, on a cold night it also provided warmth. I started to stomp my feet to get some feeling back in my legs. Then I rocked with my arms crossed to warm up my core. I glanced up just in time to see three other girls stomping their feet and rocking just like me. I tried to explain that I wasn't dancing, and that I was freezing, but it got lost in translation. I might have created a new Chinese dance move that night. Eventually Keiz made her way back to me and we both shuffled back to our apartment building.

The rest of the year consisted of roof-top and lobby dance parties depending upon the weather. When I re-upped for another year, part of me was eager to see what new boundaries I'd be willing to push. Dancing was becoming addicting, like a runner who misses running or a person who needs "just one more" tattoo. It wasn't an easy feeling to define, but it made sense to me.

My second year, there were a lot of teachers eager to dance and strut their stuff for Culture Week. I thought I'd earned a bit of a break and signed up to work the lights for American night. But there was still the dancing itch, and Asia Night scratched it. Joe—an American-born Filipino—was working on a *tinikling* dance routine. The traditional dance of the Philippines requires quick feet and bamboo poles. It reminded me a little of the rubber band Chinese jump rope, but a misstep with the bamboo poles left bruises, not rope burns.

We took turns doing the stepping and clapping. The clapping was easier for me than the stepping. The hardest part of clapping was getting a grip on the massive bamboo poles with my stubby fingers. After that, it was as simple as one, two, three. Holding the poles shoulder-width apart, my partner and I would clap the poles on the ground on a count of "one" and "two," and then bring them together on "three." One, two, clap, one, two, clap, echoed throughout the fifth floor lobby and hallways. The barefoot dancers joined in and added their own melody. One, thump, two, thump, clap, thump, one, thump, two, thump, clap, *ooouch*. Only soccer and football players suffered more injuries than the *tinikling* dancers.

Initially, I was learning the dance for my own enjoyment and self-education, but injuries pulled me off the sidelines and into the frontline once again for Culture Week. It was a much calmer night. No lines to learn, no dance steps to remember, just counting. Kelly and I handled the bamboo, while Joe and Lindsay did the fancy footwork. Aside from kneeling on the cold marble stage, it was my best night of public dancing.

If I could have stopped there, life in China would have been pretty good. But I didn't stop there. I allowed myself to be talked into participating in several more dances, each one bigger and more elaborate than the last. It never failed after each performance: I'd swear off dancing ever again, and then as soon as the next dance was announced, I was all in. At first I thought dance was filling a void left behind from my active athletics days, but I played ultimate Frisbee, volleyball, and basketball with my friends, so that wasn't it. I wracked my brain trying to figure out why I kept joining the madness, and the only answer I kept coming up with was that I liked doing it. It didn't make any sense to me at all, but it was true. In those moments when I was able to get to a point where I could let go, it was the greatest feeling in the world. Total unabashed freedom.

But as with all things in life, freedom has a price. I paid in blisters, sweat, and frustration. Seriously how hard is it to count to eight? For this journalism major, pretty hard. Thankfully, the next dance featured moves that were easier for me to learn and introduced me to Daft Punk. For several weeks, I worked on getting *Harder, Better, Faster, Stronger* for the homecoming ceremony. Joe and Heather worked out the choreography, then had the daunting task of teaching it to twenty-odd individuals, whose skill levels ranged from non-existent to amazing. I was nominal, at best. The choreography was easy and didn't require me to make too many uncomfortable undulations—and when it was called for, I was tucked away in the back, away from prying eyes. Fittingly, the last move of the dance was to collapse onto the stage. I half plopped down on the wooden stage out of exhaustion and half from exuberance. I had let myself go. I made mistakes—which can still be seen on YouTube—but I had the time of my life. My addiction was growing.

In addition to gaining confidence, I was bolstered in the summer of 2008 by the release of *Mamma, Mia!* I am not ashamed to say that I enjoy ABBA. I listened to the soundtrack over and over on Pandora or Spotify, and dreamed that I was the dancing queen. Even in the car, I had to dance to it. It's possible fellow travelers thought I'd been taken over by some alien being. I returned to China for year three ready to take on all-comers. If Pierce Brosnan could do it, so could I. Luckily for me, my fellow teachers had also fallen in love with the film. We watched it numerous times. When assigning roles—it was sort of a game that we'd assign characters to ourselves from each movie as we watched—I, naturally, was pegged as Rosie, the short, feisty writer. (I could live with that.)

As Culture Week preparations started, I thought about joining team Europe in hopes of a *Mamma, Mia!* parody. However, I decided to go with team Asia again and was delighted to be part of an *Aladdin* reboot. Instead of finding suitors for the princess, our tale centered on finding a princess for the prince. And like all good Chinese productions, it would be full of dancing and young love. Our show did not disappoint, and the princesses from various Asian countries vied for the prince by performing traditional dances. I played two roles: The queen and the safety marshal. The first was much easier.

While I had spent my summer chilling by the pool and watching movies, my buddy, Kat, had been traveling around Thailand and learned the art of fire dancing. She decided to work it into her act, which was awesome and scary all at the same time. She had non-flammable practice gear, which was impressive to watch by itself. But she had to design her own flammable gear. Yes, you can get fireworks the size of your head in Henan, but you cannot find fire dancing equipment. Several trips to fabric stores, hardware stores and other odd places netted the desired results. I was super scared the first time she lit them. I wouldn't let her try without buckets of water and sand at the ready to put the flames out. She handled the fire and my paranoia like a pro, keeping both in check. Each practice session went without incident, and although I knew the danger was still real, my apprehension was much less. However, the buckets were still ready.

As the queen, I had more lines and less dancing with this production. My only dancing would be part of the mass finale dance which would combine steps from each of the various princess' dances. I felt confident I could get those steps down in time. I was less confident when Joe informed me that the king and queen would do a short stroll down to the front. My apprehension was soon erased when he informed me that they had decided to do the final number to ABBA's song, and I would be a true dancing queen.

Best. News. Ever.

It was nearly too much. It was about that time that Paul's word's came back to me, "You're God's favorite." I sure felt like it right about then.

Joe, ever the patient teacher, made the strolling light and easy for me. I was so excited about the music and dancing that performing in the front row was nearly lost on me. The night of the performance was true joy. To share the stage with my dear friends, to watch all their hard work result in amazing dances, and to be in the moment was truly one of the best times of my life—and easily one of the best Culture Week moments. Kat's fire dance went off without a hitch, the prince picked the servant girl with the heart of gold, the students applauded wildly, and I danced with my king and *for* my King.

I was starting to understand that when the Bible talked about doing all for God, that it really meant *all*. It wasn't just about things I'd classified as deep or spiritual. But I could honestly dance, play, and laugh all for God, and He would be there with me.

CHAPTER 10

BALLIN' LIKE A GIRL

The classroom wasn't the only place I found myself confused during my tenure in China. I also found myself shaking my head in disbelief in places where I typically felt very at home—such as the basketball court.

When I was lucky enough to be part of a pick-up game between the foreign teachers, the game felt very familiar: I'd sit on the bench, go in for a bit, pass the ball to the tall people, high-five them after they scored, and run back on defense. The last time I was effective on the basketball court was when Ronald Reagan was in his *first* term in office. At least in high school, I was on a fairly even playing field with girls my own age. Playing with the foreign faculty, not only was I one of the shortest, but I was also one of the oldest. Toss in the co-ed aspect, and well, yeah, I was a solid cheerleader from the bench.

It was a bit different when it was just the female faculty. The average height came down several inches, but the age gap was the same. The nice thing was my fellow female ballers appreciated the fundamentals of the game, which meant my abilities to set a pick, make the back-door pass, and take a charge counted for something.

My b-ball buddies were Sarah G. (aka "G") and Ruth. G was everything I was not on the court: skilled, athletic, and quiet. Ruth, a recent graduate of Virginia Tech, was the first person I ever met who was excited to learn that I had covered the WNBA as a sports reporter. We talked for hours about the Sacramento Monarchs' Ticha Penicheiro and Ruthie Bolton. I'll admit I was shocked that anyone outside of the capital city had heard of the team.

While teaching in China brought us together, basketball united us in a way only sport can. There is a common vocabulary, shared passion, and kindred spirit. Plus, it's basketball—America's game, and it's quickly becoming China's. The majority of my students participated in club soccer teams, but they took the names of NBA players for their English names. Even the girls. My students' knowledge of United States geography was not vast but they could locate Los Angeles (Lakers), Houston (Rockets), Miami (Heat), Boston (Celtics), New York (Nets) and Philadelphia (Sixers)—which was three more than the Chinese cities I could locate.

Our university had a great men's team that competed in the Chinese University Basketball Association (CUBA—yeah, that acronym caused a few puzzled looks down the road). On the flipside, there wasn't a women's team…or if there was, the school kept it under deep wraps. There were student club teams for soccer, basketball, and tennis, and they played at various courts around campus. The majority of them were, again, male. To set the record straight, I would be the last person tapped as a feminist, but even I had a sense that this was unfair. Let's blame my increasing sense of injustice on growing up with Title IX and the idea that boys and girls sports should be even. FYI, there is no Title IX in China.

To fill the void, G and Ruth decided that women's basketball would make a great after-class English Corner. In addition to teaching and participating in Culture Week, the university asked foreign faculty to host English Corners. These after-hours programs could be on any subject, and were designed to get students extra time with foreign teachers to hopefully gain extra time to practice their English skills. The Corners were as varied as the teaching staff: Acoustic guitar, cooking, Scrabble, idioms, etc. G and Ruth led the Corner and asked me to help. How could I say no? It was basketball, and meant that I didn't need to run a Corner on my own. It was a win-win. As the leader of the group, G dealt with the higher ups in administration to get us time in the gymnasium.

When G met with Those In Charge, they basically said the group could meet outside. (The men's teams needed to be inside at *all* available hours.) That didn't set well with any of us. G pushed until the Powers That Be relented and signed official papers giving the women the right to meet in the gym for an hour of basketball practice. Before celebrating a major breakthrough in women's rights, having a paper saying you can do something and actually doing it are two very different things. This dichotomy cost me hours of sleep while living overseas and caused numerous headaches. China's track record with the treatment of its people is far from perfect, and even more so when it comes to women. This has nurtured generations of pragmatic people.

We had told the women the English Corner would be at the gymnasium and that they should meet us there. When we arrived, the students were giddy with excitement. I asked them why they were so happy.

"We've never been able to play in the gym before," said one, who was so excited she couldn't stop bouncing on her toes.

"Never?"

Nope, never. It was for the men. The women *had* been inside to cheer the men's team, but never to play or practice. This was the way of things. They hadn't even thought to try.

Upon arriving we found the gym occupied with the men's basketball team. G showed them the official papers, which they basically laughed at and told us to be on our way. They did not get off the court. We practiced outside. The women didn't really react to being turned away—we foreigners were a tad miffed. It was the way it had been, and the way it would continue.

Many of those first meetings were outside as we found the gym occupied or locked. The women were happy just to be learning about basketball. The Americans were starting to get annoyed—and there are few things to be feared more than annoyed American women.

G continued to push and work the system until finally we were allowed in the gym. The men's team walked slowly off the court like they'd just lost a championship at the buzzer as the women giggled and took the floor.

It was not my first time in the gym. As a foreign teacher—despite being a woman—I had been inside numerous times for pick-up basketball games and badminton. As gymnasiums go, this one was old, like dribble-killing-dead-spots-on-the-floor old. But by the women's reactions you would have thought we were at Madison Square Garden.

Ruth led the stretching exercises, which always started out as a lesson in how to make a circle. It was important for us that not only did the women practice English, but that they learn proper techniques and fundamentals. They had been taught to bounce when stretching. We convinced them to take it slow and steady. Their overall ball-handling skills were "learned" from watching ESPN highlights and the occasional Houston Rockets' Yao

Ming highlight segment on CCTV. Which is to say, they were seconds of flash followed by many minutes of fizzle.

As a sixth grader, I learned three basic passes: Bounce, chest, and baseball. (For my non-sports friends reading this: A bounce pass hits the floor before reaching your teammate, a chest pass is used for close passes that don't touch the floor, and a baseball pass is when you lean back and throw it far down the court.) I dribbled, with blinders, left- and right-handed around chairs. I worked on shooting form, practiced countless free throws and layups. If I took a shot more than two feet from the paint, my coach would berate me in front of my teammates and ask why I was trying to showboat. I thought these were things that everyone learned in sixth grade. I was wrong.

Most of that first day inside was spent on passing and dribbling. It was not pretty. I must confess that several of my passes went through student's hands and ricocheted off their chests or faces. I felt horrible and—truth be told—annoyed that a twenty-two-year-old woman had never had the chance to learn how to properly pass and receive a bounce pass.

Shooting produced more of the same. They all wanted to shoot from downtown, which made for a lot of air balls. We ran them through layups, free throws, and some baseline and elbow shooting drills. The influence of TV was evident as they quickly stopped doing what they'd just learned and try outlandish moves they had seen Tracy McGrady or Kobe Bryant make in a game.

It took several more English Corners for the women to find their rhythm, but find it they did. We started having more scrimmages and fewer balls to the face. Just when we had the higher ups on board with the female students in the gym, the foreign female teachers were suddenly on the outs. In years past, a co-ed foreign faculty team had taken on local officials in a "friendly" basketball game. The team the year before us featured an outstanding female faculty member, who helped the international squad upset the locals despite questionable officiating. This year, they took no chances, and women were not allowed to play. I was pretty sure that at five-foot-one-ish, I was not going to be asked to play anyway, but having the option taken away made it extra infuriating. So, I sat in the stands and cheered on the foreign faculty in a losing effort that we all knew was coming.

It was a brutal loss. Not so much on the scoreboard, but mentally and physically. There are few things more frustrating than having rules ignored or only enforced against you. I was proud that the foreign teachers were able to keep their cool ninety-nine percent of the time. I knew it was tough on them, but had no real idea until I found myself in their high tops.

Every year, there was a major club basketball tournament on campus that featured teams of students and faculty with the final pairing featuring the top student and faculty team. The first few years, the foreign women's teams easily dominated—well, not easily. When we played our first game, it was obvious our counterparts did not have the same early childhood hoops training that we enjoyed. My junior high and high school experiences taught me that basketball is the most physical, non-contact sport around. I was used to being jostled and bounced around, but that was nothing compared to the muggings and huggings—yes, really—I encountered in that rickety old gym.

Since we played woman-on-woman, we picked our person to guard just before the tipoff, just like any other game I've played. We won the tip, and I moved over to be a wing. Next thing I knew a defender wrapped her arms all the way around me. I looked at the referee, who didn't seem bothered by it at all. I looked around and all of us were being hugged. We tried to make a case for this being a foul, but it fell on deaf ears. One of my teammates had two girls corralling her. Forget a moving screen, this was a moving fence. My favorite moment came after we scored and I ran back for defense, my defender again wrapped me in a bear hug. I was so confused.

"I'm on defense now," I said.

She continued to hold on.

"You should let go of me, and go get the ball to shoot," I said. "You're offense now."

Granted this may have been more effective had I been able to say all this in Mandarin.

I pointed at her player with the ball, hoping this would trigger a release button. She looked back, smiled as her teammate scored and let go briefly to cheer. I took advantage of the situation to run freely to the other end. Running, sadly, was what I was in for that night.

With no help from the referees, our only option was to just speed up and not let them catch us. We built a steady lead with layups and put backs. At one point I was so mentally fatigued, I thought we must be losing only to look at the score table and see we were well ahead. Not wanting to rub it in, we slowed the game and again were back into wrap-up mode.

Ruth and G headed back to life in America, and in my third year I was tapped as the faculty women's player/coach. I'll admit I was a tad worried that without G and Ruth we were in for a rough go of it. However, our rag-tag band of misfits—Kat, Lindsay, Kinah, Willson, Stacie, and Annie—proved more than capable.

The player/coach role was new to me, and took some time to find the right balance. I wanted to be on the court the whole time, but I knew that was silly when I had younger, able-bodied teammates. Kat and Lindsay took care of most of the scoring; Stacie and Willson—I've always called her by her family name instead of Sarah—controlled the inside; and Kinah, Annie, and I took turns at the point.

I don't remember laughing so much on and off the court with teammates. It took Kinah awhile to get the handle of dribbling and running. More often than not, she picked up the basketball and just ran with it. As in previous years, we built early leads despite being constantly fouled and were able to play fairly stress-free.

We collected our hardware at the end of the tournament: Champions of all China. Well, at least Henan. Okay, Xinzheng. It was a great feeling. Not just the winning, but also the camaraderie. It was more than recapturing glory days. It was stepping out of the box and trying new things. It was rediscovering the joy of being on the floor with teammates and encouraging each other and making each other better.

The sad thing about feelings is that they change.

During my time playing in China against the local faculty, I received countless elbows to the head, neck and stomach areas, and was rewarded with bloody noses and a pair of broken glasses. My final year was the hardest. We had won each of the preceding years. This year, our team was not as strong, and I lacked the gumption to create a solid practice schedule. We were beaten, badly. *I* was beaten, badly. And I behaved badly. I argued calls—again knowing the language would have helped. Adding insult to injury, while most of the women's teams still played the grab-and-don't-let-go style, the physical education teams started using plays. They used our game against us. Four years prior with G and Ruth, I would have been up to the challenge. But after years of grinding out against a stacked deck, I was done. They had found a way to beat me—on and off the scoreboard. China and its dominating ways are a major machine that just wears you down until loss is acceptable.

More than losing on the scoreboard, I hated the feeling of losing my integrity. I hated that something I enjoyed doing had turned into such an enormous chore. I fell head-over-heels for China when I arrived in 2006, and now, midway through my fifth year, I was starting to feel the needle turn toward ire. I knew it would be my last year. China teaches you to be pragmatic that way.

Less than forty-eight hours into my first adventure into China and I'm standing on the Great Wall. It had been raining all day, but stopped for the hour I meandered Mutianyu.

The entrance to The Forbidden City is across from Tiananmen Square. Like all the other tourists, I had to get my picture taken with the famous Chairman Mao Zedong portrait.

I met these beautiful grandmas on my first bike ride through the village behind the university. I chatted with them a few minutes and even got invited to lunch (I think).

It's my first day of teaching. I was excited, and a bit nervous, but with my good-luck red jacket, I couldn't be stopped.

In the spring and fall, the Sias University campus was lush and green. The main classroom buildings were set up in a massive oval in the center of campus.

When I wasn't exploring on my own, students would set up times for all of us to go bike riding together. This is a mix of students from my first year's classes.

I was all about the California beach culture my first Culture Week. I had two massive surfboards cut out of thick boards and then painted them. Students enjoyed taking their pictures with them.

God bless Heather (left) and Autumn (right) for all their patience in teaching me (middle) how to line dance. It wasn't pretty, but I eventually figured it out.

My first hike of the ancestral mountain Shizuishan, just outside of Xinzheng, was a great adventure. It was also one of the clearest days, and the sky could actually be called blue.

Fellow teacher Christa and I are flanked by our students at the top of the mountain.

Being born in the year of the goat, seemed only appropriate to take a picture with one.

I visited the amazing city of Xi'An several times. My first year, I went on the university sponsored trip that, for a slight fee, included a tour of Qin Shi Huang's formidable terracotta warriors.

The Wenfeng Pagoda is a popular place to visit in Anyang. It wasn't an easy climb up the wonky stone steps. My tall friend hit her head, while I bonked my knees.

My first Chinese grandma and I around the table for a light snack during Spring Festival in Anyang.

Mom and Dad taking their first step on the Great Wall at Badaling.

My parents and Julian pose for a picture at the entrance to the Shaolin Temple area.

My parents follow behind us on the chairlift at the Shaolin Temple.

Mom and Dad stop for a picture in front of the Asian side of the Sias University administration building. The other side, on the inside of the campus, is modeled after Washington, D.C. buildings.

One of the happiest and proudest days as a teacher and friend was watching those first classes I taught graduate. Four of the Six Pack (Jack, Kevin, Michael, and Julian) found me after the ceremony for a fun picture.

Surprise! The Six Pack took me out to dinner, days before my birthday, for a surprise birthday party. Pictured are Michael, Kevin, Sue, me, and Julian, who deemed my cake cutting skills to be lacking.

Annabelle and Uncle's Uncle prepare to lead the way to the ancestral burial site in Feng Zhuang Village in Bo'Ai County.

The hanging of the Spring Festival couplets is a major part of celebrating Spring Festival. These were painted by one of Annabelle's uncles, hung up by Brother (black coat) under the supervision of Annabelle, far left, me, and Cousin.

The street that Annbelle and her family have lived on for multiple generations.

The double-trouble tandem of Eileen and Annabelle blow bubbles in the park during Spring Festival.

Kat and I were two of the shorter teachers at Sias. However, together we impressed members of the Chinese University Basketball Association women's championship team.

My third year in Xinzheng, many bike rentals added motorized scooters. I spent many weekends zooming around town, and, usually, Sarah was with me.

The Shaolin monks' cemetery is sometimes referred to as a pagoda forest. The more revered the monk, the higher his burial pagoda.

They started building a Three-Self Church across the street from the university my second year. Once it was finished, it held Chinese services Sunday mornings, followed by a foreigner-led Power Hour for students to experience a Western religious service.

I had a lot of fun my first two years with Shellie and Ruthie, including traveling to Shanghai to watch the Women's World Cup finals.

My fourth Culture Week experience included fulfilling the dream of being a literal dancing queen, thanks to my buddy Joe. We borrowed the bling for free from a local store.

CHAPTER 11

THE THREE-SELF CHURCH: ME, MYSELF, AND I

It's pretty easy to feel paranoid living in a strange place. It's extremely easy living in a communist state that is known for invasions of privacy. One of my friends disassembled his phone after he heard beeps during a conversation. He never put it back together just in case "they" were listening.

That first year, nearly every conversation with Chinese faculty or students felt like a test, especially, talks dealing with religion. I knew it was okay for me to answer questions, but I was a bit nervous about why the questions were being asked.

"You are a Christian?" asked a student whose name I hadn't yet memorized during my first office hours. It was phrased as a question, but delivered more as a statement. I made a quick scan of the handful of students sitting in my living room. All of them were doing little head bobs.

"Yes," I said, maybe too hesitantly. I wasn't ashamed of my faith, but I wasn't so sure secret police weren't going to come busting through my door.

"We know this," the student continued. "All of our American teachers are."

Again, heads bobbed all around.

I found this odd—the statement, not the agreement—because I knew there were numerous non-Christians on the staff because they were vocal in their dislike of believers.

"All of your teachers?" I asked.

"No," she said. "All the Americans. All Americans are Christians."

The wave of bobbing continued.

In a country where "saving face" or *guanxi* is so important, I wasn't sure how to address the inaccuracy while not causing my student to be shamed in front of her peers. It was a tightrope I eventually became very good at walking.

"That's interesting. Can you tell me where you learned this fact?" I asked. "It's a bit different than what I know from living there."

She explained that various textbooks and Chinese professors stated that America is a Christian nation, all Americans are Christians and want to make China the same. This time I joined in on the head bobbing.

"Kinda, sorta."

"What is meaning?"

Many a conversation mutated into a grammar or English lesson as I forgot my students, while proficient in English, were not masters of slang, idioms, conjunctions, etc.

"I understand how professors could reach that conclusion," I started, tiptoeing on that wire, "but America has changed a great deal. There are people of every religion and some with no religion. There are Christians in America; but not all Americans are Christian."

Heads stopped bobbing and pivoted to their spokesperson.

"But you are a Christian," she stated with a hint of question in her tone.

"Yes."

This restarted the bobbleheads.

"Okay," she said. "May I ask another question?"

"Sure," I said bracing and preparing for more theology questions.

"How old are you and why are you not married?"

I was preparing to say, that's two questions and not typically asked of women, when the girl on the end of the couch piped up.

"You are not to ask Teacher her age," she said. "It is not polite."

"Thank you," I said, and reminded all the girls that they were allowed to call me Kim. "I don't mind, but other women may take offense."

"I am sorry."

"It's okay. I'm thirty-nine, and I like the freedom of being single."

There were gasps and muted conversations in Mandarin.

In a country where women were expected to be married by twenty-four, my middle-aged singleness was shocking.

"Do you have any other questions for me?"

All of them shook their heads.

"No, Teacher. Our time is up. We will go now."

They said their polite goodbyes and left me wondering what had just happened.

Nearly the exact same scene played out over the following office hours with the next class. However, I noted an interesting phenomenon when my third class came to visit. They had obviously talked with the previous students because this group was savvy on not only what not to ask, but also that not all Americans were Christians.

This lulled me into thinking that future conversations would be about English and classwork. Over the course of five years, maybe ten percent of office hours were spent on class topics.

Conversations tended to steer back to religion. I let my students take the wheel because if it was a trap I didn't want to drive myself to jail.

I got the attraction. As a communist nation, China's government was atheist at its core. Then when the Bamboo Curtain came down, trade went up, and the nation trended toward communism with socialist tendencies and even added some capitalism in the mix. In the process, to avoid staying on numerous watch lists, the country now had freedom of religion. Granted, it's a very limited freedom with Christianity, Islam and Judaism, but it exists.

For Chinese Christians, there is the Three-Self Church. Its principle trio are self-governance, self-support, and self-propagation. It is a state-run institution, so everything is pre-approved. The vast majority of those who attend these churches are the elderly who were Christians before communists closed the country. There is an innate curiosity for members of the younger generation when they encounter someone or something they don't see all the time. Me being a blonde, blue-eyed believer in central China counted as something not seen all the time.

While I was answering my student's questions with as much care as I could, it was one of my California tabletop books that caused me trouble and had me searching my gray matter for church history answers. There was a picture of one of California's twenty-one missions. Its bright white adobe walls covered in bougainvillea stood in stark contrast to the cloudless azure sky. They knew it was a church from the cross, but it was an unfamiliar architectural style.

"Teacher, is this your church?"

"Nope, it's a mission."

Blank stares.

"It was a Catholic church built hundreds of years ago," I further explained. "The church built them up the California coast to colonize the native people, and they were built like a day's walk apart for safety."

"You are not Catholic?"

"No, I'm Protestant."

Blank stares and head tilts.

"I thought you were Christian," inquired one student I wasn't even sure spoke English.

"Ha, yeah, I am," I said, as it dawned on me these were new concepts to them. "Protestant and Catholic are both Christian. They have different views on how to practice their faiths."

I wasn't prepared to go through the entirety of Martin Luther and his excommunication and all that followed (ironically, it was covered in our reading textbook later that semester and by me in the following chapter). I hoped that answer would suffice.

It did and it didn't.

They then started to ask if Teacher so-and-so was also Protestant. Not wanting to out my fellow teachers, I walked the high wire by turning the question back on them.

"Did they tell you about their religion?"

"Yes, they are Baptists."

"Gotcha. I used to be Baptist, but I'd identify more now as Pentecostal."

It is hard to categorize their facial expressions other than perplexed. Their worldviews were being turned upside down.

"So you were Christian then Protestant then Baptist and now something else?"

"No, I've been a Christian since I was a kid," I said slowly, giving myself time to formulate my answer. "While there are two major rules for being a Christian—love God, love your neighbor—there are also a lot of other rules that some do or do not follow and that breaks down Catholic, Baptist, Evangelical, Lutheran…"

With each sect I added to the list, their glances between each other grew. I was not helping the situation. I suddenly envied the Three-Self Church and Chinese Christians who didn't have to deal with denominations and fractures of faith.

It was in my first semester abroad, away from the mega-church I had called home for decades, away from friends' and families' beliefs, away from the infighting of American believers, that I was able to find faith on my own terms.

I dropped the assigned sub-label of denomination and just held on to Christianity and pursued the Father, Son, and Holy Spirit the best way I could in a communist country with socialist tendencies. Ironically, it was a way better way.

Since there wasn't a church building for foreigners in our city, we did what the original church did and created a community of believers. We would meet in various places for many reasons. Sometimes it was like a traditional church service with singing, praying, and a message. Sometimes it was sharing testimonies and encouraging words. Sometimes it was just singing or praying. But it was always open to any foreigner regardless of their assigned denomination.

Sadly, but not unexpected, our community had fractures. The major split was along traditional lines. The traditionalists viewed our campus as an extension of their churches in the States, and wanted to adhere to those rules. They objected to our allowing women—shocking—to deliver a message and the free flowing movement of the Spirit.

For me, it felt confining to attend services led by traditionalists, but I'd go. I loved singing old hymns and being with my friends.

It was rare for the visits to go the other way. One forever burned in my brain was when one of the teachers that I'd known from day one slipped quietly through the curtain and was standing in the back. (Yes, technically, I should have been facing front and singing.)

My heart was so happy when I saw him. I thought, "Yes, he'll see the freedom and feel the Spirit and want to join in with us." In less than a minute, I saw the countenance of his face change and he spun around and walked out.

We continued to be friends, but I could tell there was something different. I was so conflicted. How could I be learning to walk in freedom, while others appeared to cling tighter to their bonds? (In all fairness, in reflection, I understand each person takes their own stand. However, at the time, I wanted everyone to experience the same thing as I.)

In the years that followed, a legit Three-Self Church was built right across the street from our campus. It was, in all honesty, one of the gaudiest buildings around. Thankfully, inside it just looked like a building.

The traditional front established what they called "Power Hour" on Sundays at the church. The proposal stated this was a chance for the students to have an American experience. And in keeping with their ideals, it was a traditional experience.

As with the activities in our community, I enjoyed the singing and being in community at Power Hour. But with its expansive ceiling and massive interior, I felt like I was back in California attending a mega-service. The message always ended with a question for the students to ask their teachers about their faith. I didn't like the feeling of forced evangelism. Having grown up during the time of Billy Graham, I was very aware that this is how services were supposed to end. But I didn't like it. I preferred more natural means of reaching deep conversation, ones where my actions inspired true and organic inquiries. Thankfully, I had a few of those.

One night, a handful of us were out on the town having dinner. Away from class, Americans had a reputation for being loud, and I and my friends could bring the noise. We were enjoying our dinner, laughing and the lot.

As we were leaving, one of my students stopped me. This was not unusual. Despite being a city of more than 900,000 people, Xinzheng was small. And the number of restaurants frequented by foreigners was even smaller.

"Good evening, Teacher, may I ask you a question?"

"Yes, and remember you can call me Kim."

"Yes, Teacher. Why are you and your friends so?"

I was waiting for a word to follow "so," but that was it.

"So, how?"

"When we are with our friends it is not the same. There is something about you and your friends together that is different."

I am never so happy to be called "different" than when it comes to my faith. My hope is people see authenticity and unconditional love. That night my student and her friends saw enough to know what genuine friendship looks like. It opened a door for me to share my faith and tell her where my ability to care for others comes from and let her know it's not limited to Americans.

During my time in China, I had several talks about faith with students and friends. I was careful then—and continue today because a little paranoia is good—to not share names of individual believers. Christians in the underground church have been and continue to be arrested and thrown in prison for their beliefs that exist outside the Three-Self Church.

Thanks to my students, friends, and government regulations, my faith grew, was challenged and flourished. Many times since returning to the United States, I have longed for the simplicity of my time in China, but I know that life's current challenges will only refine it and me even more.

KIM ORENDOR

CHAPTER 12

MARTIN LUTHER, THE PENTECOSTAL MOVEMENT, AND THE HOLOCAUST

T he ironic thing about being a teacher is that you tend to learn more from a lesson than your students. And when you're teaching in a foreign country, you tend to learn a lot about yourself and that one lesson does not fit all cultures.

As I forced myself to get out of my comfort zone and onto the dance floor, I was trying to push the limits on teaching as well. I thought back to all the teachers I had endured and thrived under, and tried to pick and choose what parts I wanted to incorporate into my style of teaching. In addition, my brain was still very aware of the difficulty of learning a foreign language. I wanted to try and add an element of fun to classes, if for nothing else than to keep the students awake. This was not always successful, but I learned to not take it personally.

The university provided textbooks for my reading classes. The journalism book had relevant vocabulary, but was filled with dated copy and cumbersome examples. I had fifteen years of journalism experience under my belt, and even I was bewildered by some sections. I knew it would cause extreme confusion in the minds of second-language learners. To ensure that the majority of us enjoyed the semester, I kept the vocabulary to establish a base language and then pretty much ignored the book and taught from experience.

The comprehensive reading textbook posed a conundrum all its own. It had three sections with religious themes: Martin Luther, the Pentecostal Movement, and the Holocaust. I felt as if the administration was setting me up. If I closed my eyes and listened intently, I swear I could hear Admiral Ackbar screaming, "It's a trap." All my pre-China training taught me to avoid religion and the three Ts—Taiwan, Tiananmen, and Tibet—in the classroom. And now, it was in my textbook. Part of me relished the idea of talking about Martin Luther and the idea of grace, but the other part of me hated the idea of getting into the split of Catholicism and Protestantism. I'd suffered through hours and hours of Bible class in high school learning about the Reformation, the Diet of Worms (which has nothing to with calories or nightcrawlers), indulgences, and The 95 Theses. There was no way I was doing that to my students.

I racked my brain to try and figure out how a section on the Pentecostal Movement even got into the textbook. It's such a small subset of all other denominations that I figured someone who edited the book knew someone who knew someone who knew someone who said, "This is important, put this in there." Again, as a Protestant who believes in the power of the Holy Spirit, I believe the power that flowed through the New Testament Pentecost of the early apostles is the same power that sparked the movement in America. However, I was still wondering if this wasn't a ruse, and I would end up in a Chinese jail trying to defend myself with my limited Mandarin.

Apparently I was the only reading teacher with a case of paranoia. My partner teacher was extremely excited for the lessons. He saw it as a perfect opportunity for evangelism. Was I the only person who remembered signing a contract that said I wouldn't proselytize in the classroom? Usually we taught very similar lessons, but for the next three weeks I knew I was going to be on my own. To help alleviate my paranoia, I taught the Pentecostal section straight from the book. Probably the most boring lecture ever given. But that part of me that loves the idea of grace would not let Martin Luther be boring. I felt I owed him that for getting me out of indulgences.

I told my multi-denominational book club in California about the chapter a few months before I had to teach it. Page-turners Laura and Michael told me they had a DVD of the movie *Luther*, and that I could borrow it to show to my students. I jumped at the chance—I had seen the film and loved it—but sadly knew since it was a reading class that I could only show clips and not the whole film. (I did arrange for a showing of the entire film outside of class if students wanted to see it. The room was filled.) Joseph Fiennes portrayed Luther with brilliance. His facial expressions and body language were able to translate ideas to my students, who were tripping over the unfamiliar vocabulary. They watched as he entered Rome with expectation, as he is fixated with the relics and finally as he bought an indulgence and crawled up the outer steps of a church. During his ascension, he began looking around at all the people. He saw the priests collecting money, the people hawking religious trinkets, and the sea of humanity. His face hardened, then softened, and he crumpled his indulgence and dropped it.

I stopped the DVD and let the moment hang in the air. "What do you think he is feeling?"

"He looks like his heart hurts," a girl answered. I nodded in agreement.

I skipped forward to where Luther preached a message where he admitted he was wrong when he talked about God as being angry and waiting to punish people. He brought a new message to the people that said, "To see God in faith is to look upon his friendly heart." That line was so true in my own life at the time, I was finally beginning to see the Father's true heart. I wanted my students to be able to experience that also. I wanted them to know grace and freedom. But I also knew grace and freedom came with a price—especially in a communist country—and it would be students, like Luther, who would pay the heaviest price. As an American believer, the worst that people do to me is call me names. As a Chinese believer, you can be fined, jailed, and sometimes worse. My heart began to hurt.

I thought about showing *Schindler's List* in class for the Holocaust lesson, but then another idea came to me. It was an idea birthed from two different high school experiences.

My sophomore year in Missouri, I saw a television special called *The Wave*. It was based on the true story of a 1967 experiment in a California high school. In the movie, a teacher created a new movement called The Wave. Most students were drawn in by the ideals and it was pretty apparent where the show was headed. There were a couple of students who didn't agree with the movement, and they were shunned, harassed, and chased. The isolated loner found his inner bully in the dominating movement and blindly followed the teacher. The teacher—portrayed by Bruce Davison—started to buy his own fascist propaganda and then got his head on straight in time to stop things from getting too crazy. The scene burned into my brain was when the teacher told the students there would be a rally and their national leader would be speaking. The kids were all excited and filed in to see the presentation, which turned out to be footage of Adolf Hitler. They were all shocked at how they could be pulled into something so crazy. I hoped I'd never have a teacher like that, but my hope was short-lived.

I didn't expect too much boat rocking from the teachers at the small private school I attended in Northern California. They were a pretty conservative lot compared to some of public school teachers I'd had. One day, our teacher announced we were going to have a guest. This usually meant no homework, so I was excited. My excitement didn't last long. At first I really wasn't listening to her (you wouldn't have been either), but then she started talking about blonde, blue-eyed people not being as smart as other people and everyone knew that. As a blonde, blue-eyed person, I was now listening. I knew I wasn't the smartest person in our class. That honor belonged to Janet, a very blonde, very blue-eyed person. I was confused as to why our teacher allowed this lady to talk such nonsense. She continued talking—now I wasn't hearing because I was frustrated—and she broke us into groups for testing. The non-blue-eyed, blonde people made up and graded the tests, which we "stupid" people took. The questions weren't hard, but the graders never gave us credit for right answers. As my frustration level grew, I noticed others seemed okay with it and just went along. Moments from a full-scale riot from me and the other blondes who'd had enough, the lady finally got around to the point of the experiment: Knowing what it feels like to be singled out for race, creed, genetics, etc. If our class had been an actual thug state, I'd be dead—and I took satisfaction in the fact that I would have gone down fighting at least.

If two decades later those experiments stuck with me, I wanted to try something similar to make a powerful impact on my students. There were a few upfront problems that I faced: My students were more at home following a pack than rebelling, and they were all dark-haired and dark-eyed. I scoured their student information cards and determined I'd break them up by regional zones. I made a set of colored cards—red, yellow, green, blue. I then divided the classroom into study zones, each area was designated for students to work on a specific part of that week's lesson. The signs also showed which color could or could not be in that zone. Red, since it's China's lucky color, was the ultimate card. Not only could it go to any zone, but it also allowed students to ask me for answers. Yellow, the second lucky color, was the next best. Allowed at all zones but students could not ask me for help. Students with green cards were allowed at all but one zone. And maybe subconsciously because of my high school experience, blue was the lowest in the class. They were allowed in one zone only.

The hardest part for me was keeping students out of zones where they were not allowed. My favorite class of students was having a particularly difficult time, especially Michael. His blue card meant he had to stay in the back corner with the other blues. It was hot and crowded and he wanted to do other things. Every time he'd try to leave the area, I'd corral him and send him back. Some joined his dissention, but most went with the idea that teacher knows best. After several attempts to escape, Michael flopped hard into his seat.

"Kim, why are you frustrating me so?" he said as he crossed his arms and stared at me with an expression that nearly broke me.

"You have a blue card. You must stay here."

He just continued to stare at me with an I-thought-we-were-friends look. I had to turn away.

All of the lessons at various stations dealt with the Holocaust, but it wasn't until the end of the lesson that my students got the deeper meaning of the cards. I had the red, yellow, and green card holders sit at the front of the class and blues in the back. I then explained that if it had been the Holocaust, all those with blue cards would be dead simply because I decided that people from their towns were the cause of my troubles. Michael was highly distraught at being dead. I didn't much like the idea either.

I felt as if the message had come across, but teachers are instructed to ask follow-up questions to ensure the students are actually understanding.

"So what did we learn today?"

"It's not fair," said a red card girl.

"That's right," I said, thinking I was going to be up for teacher of the year. "How is it not fair?"

"I had to do everything, and the blue people did nothing."

And there goes my teacher of the year award.

Where I had thought I was showing favoritism by giving the red access to the answers and all the available points for the day, they had seen it as punishment.

It's possible Michael—one of the most tender-hearted people I've ever met—and I are the only ones who learned anything that day. My hope and prayer is that the seeds of grace, freedom, and acceptance will grow in all my students, who will pass it on to their children and produce a kinder, gentler generation.

CHAPTER 13

MAKING MYSELF AT HOME

A teaching job at Sias International University was described to me as the softest landing in China, and after talking with teachers at other universities around the province and country, it was easy to see it was a true statement.

There were more than 100 foreigners—staff and family—at Sias compared to one woman who told me she was one of two Americans. The downside was that our university didn't pay as much as other colleges, although we did enjoy numerous other perks.

Each month, the university put together a field trip to a historical site. They were all free except the overnight trip to Xi'An, the home of the terracotta warriors. We were wined and dined in the best restaurants and traveled in a comfortable bus.

Every place we visited, nearly every step we took was ordained by International Program Coordinator Charlie, the man with the travel plan. He did his best to provide western amenities for our picky bunch. He also warned of going off the beaten path and traveling too far on our own. So obviously, all of us had to get off every path and see how far we could go on our own.

I slowly widened my circle of exploration. First, it was the five-minute bike ride to downtown Xinzheng. Then, I joined some friends on the thirty-minute bus ride to nearby Zhengzhou, a city of nearly ten million people. We spent the day shopping in stores with western food items, and then grabbed a soft-serve cone at McDonalds.

I was feeling pretty good about myself and my boundary pushing. That all changed when my friend Heather asked if I'd go with her on a student home visit for Chinese New Year, aka Spring Festival.

Several foreigner teachers had shared their experiences with me about what it was like to see the "real" China by staying with a student. My non-fluent Mandarin self was nervous to go alone, but was emboldened by the prospect of traveling with a friend. Heather's student, Linda, lived in the northern reaches of the Henan Province in the ancient city of Anyang. The amazing book *Oracle Bones* by Peter Hessler is partly set in this city. It was my first time taking a train in China. Along the way, Linda taught us how to play Chinese poker. If we were betting, I'd be broke and Heather would be in first class.

When we finally reached the city, it was very late and very dark. The scarcity of street lights was a bit concerning to my western way of thinking. My paranoia peaked as taxi after taxi refused to take us to our destination. Finally, one agreed and we began our trek through an ever narrowing maze of gated walls.

"We have arrived," said Linda, at a gate that looked exactly like the last twenty we'd passed. However, we really hadn't "arrived." We still had to walk down a long dark alley, the kind you see in movies and know that person shouldn't go down. At the end of the alley was another large metal door. Linda gave it a good pounding, and soon, we were greeted by her mom and dad.

The two-story home was built within four large walls. The main gate opened to a courtyard that housed stairs, a pantry, a storage room and the squatty potty. The first floor living area consisted of a sitting room, a kitchen, and three bedrooms: One for Linda, one for her brother, and one for her parents. Linda gave up her room for us and moved in with her parents for a few days. The second floor had two empty rooms and a balcony that overhung part of the courtyard.

After quick pleasantries, we were shown to our room. The only source of heating in the home was the stove in the sitting room. Thankfully, the family—probably fearing we'd freeze to death—supplied us with a heating pad. While it was way too small to actually warm us or the bed, we used it as a pajama warmer. Heather and I wrapped ourselves up like two burritos in the bedding and stared at the ceiling.

"You awake?" I asked.

"Yes."

"You cold? I can see my breath."

"Yeah, me too."

It would have been easy to just lie there and complain, but we switched to remembering good things about that day. The smooth train ride, learning poker, Linda's English, and realized that we had a lot to be grateful for. We awoke to a cold, but clear New Year's Eve. Linda had the day planned and we followed her lead.

"We have arrived" with Linda at the most amazing street omelet food stall. A lot of people visiting China were put off by the "unsanitary" conditions. For the record, I got food poisoning once and it was in the foreign teacher apartment building's kitchen. Aside from stinky tofu, I didn't meet street food I didn't enjoy.

We also swung by the markets to pick up meats and vegetables for the meal. There are some meat staples unique to Asia that many Americans find gross and inhumane. Linda was also aware of this and before ordering the family's traditional fare of canine asked us if we would be offended. We both said, "no." Yes, I have eaten dog, along with eel, donkey, fish, chicken, veal, pork, etc. The thing I ate the least in China was beef because of its high price.

After forcing down a less-than-pleasant "beef" stew for lunch, we came across a street vendor with what at first looked like vanilla ice cream with cherries on a stick. (All good food comes on a stick.) Looking to erase the bad memory and taste of lunch, I was game for anything.

Turns out it was sticky rice and sliced haw apples, which are like a little crab apple. On their own, the fruit is twist-your-face tart, but candied, it was actually enjoyable. The "dessert" was hard-packed into a giant meatloaf pan, and plopped onto the counter, where it was sliced to order and skewered. (It tasted very similar to a sweet congee or rice pudding.)

With my stomach and head now in the right state of being, we set off for the serious work of getting the fireworks for the evening's celebration. It should be noted that "safe and sane" appeared nowhere on any pyrotechnic.

The firework stands sold everything from Roman candles to 1,000-round firecrackers. There were also M80s—originally designed to simulate explosives for U.S. military training—and what appeared to be full sticks of dynamite. One firework was bigger than my hand. They also had rounds for firework launchers like you see at major New Year's celebrations. All legal. All cheap.

Upon returning to the house—which was extremely easier during the light of day—we were met with a feast. There were plates with thinly sliced meats and a variety of veggies. I quickly became addicted to the chilled cucumbers and garlic with mushrooms and *bok choy* a close second, as well as *jiaozi* (dumplings) for days. The massive spread of food was prepped by Linda's mom and grandma. And grandma made it her mission to make sure I sampled everything…twice. Every time I cleared off my plate, she used her chopsticks to refill it. I felt as if I would explode.

"Stop eating it," Heather deftly whispered.

"Huh."

"If you keep cleaning it off, she's going to keep filling it. She thinks you're still hungry."

With my mother's mantra of, "Clean your plate; there are children starving," resonating in my head, I put my chopsticks down with food left on my plate. Grandma smiled. My stomach smiled, too, if that was even possible.

The party moved to the second floor balcony. The fireworks were spread out, and soon our explosions joined the growing cacophony in the city. I'm not sure technically how far I could see, but if it was miles, then for miles in all directions the sky was lit up in reds, greens, and blues.

As the time inched toward midnight, the sounds intensified, and firework hues were hidden behind smoky clouds. The thirty-minute stretch surrounding midnight rivaled any war movie explosions I've seen. I had never heard anything that loud in all my life.

Horrifyingly, it was topped fewer than five hours later.

At 4:30 that morning—what has lovingly become known as Half Past Death—I literally bolted upright in bed (which is not easy when one is wrapped like a burrito) as the sounds of what I thought was gunfire echoed in the house. Linda's dad had lit a 1,000-round firecracker roll in the courtyard by the front door. He added a couple M80s in the mix for good luck. Once safely back in bed, the smoke and smell of gunpowder wafted through our room, and Heather and I were tired from the event. It was still hard to hear each other much less think.

"Who does that at four in the morning? *Si dian, si dian ban*?" I questioned in English and poor Mandarin.

It was about that time that both of us recalled that four (*si*) is a bad luck number because it sounds like the Chinese word for death. People avoid selected phone numbers with fours in them. When purchasing multiples of something, people will buy three or five but not four, even if that's really all they need.

Future experiences would use this moment as a baseline.

"What was it like?"

"Not even close to Half Past Death."

New Year's Day started as a blur due to the lack of sleep. That morning was spent sitting around the stove with grandma. She made me miss my own grandma. Linda's grandma had a beautiful round face full of wrinkles that covered her eyes when she smiled. With her lack of English and my poor Mandarin, we were left playing charades to try to get our stories across.

There are no fireworks following that evening's meal. Instead we took our thousand steps for good health. Linda guided us around the city and pointed out places she felt would be of interest. We reached our destination, and I was surprised by the number of people whose 1,000 steps also ended at this park. Apparently, word got out that "there were foreigners" and the students wanted to practice their English with us.

The following morning, Douglas, one of the students we met, joined us on our trip around town. It's crazy that even in a city with more than five million people it was hard to find a "stranger." Turns out Douglas was the friend of a friend of a sister's brother who knew of our university, which pretty much made him family.

We hiked the Wenfeng Pagoda and lived to tell the tale. Living in the United States, I came to take several things for granted: The sky was blue, plumbing was indoors, and stairs were a consistent height. The steps in the pagoda varied from three inches to more than a foot. At five-feet-one-inch tall, there were several steps that caused me to stand on my tiptoes and use the handrail to pull myself up.

As annoying as that was, it was less painful than Heather's trouble of being too tall and smacking her forehead on the ceiling as she stepped up. Both of us forgot our woes as we stepped out on the walkway that allowed for panoramic views of the city.

We meandered through two more city parks and finally found ourselves back home. I was exhausted and just wanted to sleep. Another big meal had me on the verge of a food coma. I was just about to call it a night, when Linda got a phone call.

One of the young men we had met the other night at the park was hosting a party for us.

"He's inviting us to dinner."

"No," Linda clarified. "He is throwing a party in your honor. It is an honor. We must go."

Not wanting the young man to lose face, off we went. When we arrived, we learned the young man was the only one of his friends who did not go off to college. Instead, he got a job out of high school. He worried his English would not be good enough for the foreigners, and then used it to give a perfect toast for us. Even better than his English were his party hosting skills, because instead of a table full of heavy foods, he had a spread of sliced melon, sunflower and pumpkins seeds, and small dough balls filled with red bean paste. I could fully partake without him losing face and my stomach exploding.

Heading back to the university the following morning was tough. Partly because I was exhausted and partly because I had really come to like Linda's family. However, I was stoked to get back and enjoy my first shower in several days. The taxi ride getting back to the train station was just as crazy as our first ride, maybe more so. This ride required us to push start it down the alley. We started laughing as we pushed and jumped into the moving vehicle as just the week before we had watched *Little Miss Sunshine*.

Aside from needing a jumpstart, our taxi was literally falling apart around us. There was a metal plate on the floor that partially covered a hole that revealed the spinning drive shaft. Our driver informed us that he could not stop, and he wasn't kidding. He made quick turns to beat lights and veered into open spaces. We laughed until we realized this meant we'd be getting out of a moving car at the train station.

Surviving Half Past Death and Mr. Toad's Wild Taxi Ride turned out to be a warmup for the train ride home. It felt as if every single person in China was on our train. Thankfully, we had assigned seats. Linda and I were together, and Heather was across the aisle. This was not a problem at first. However, the train also sold standing-room-only tickets. Do you know how many Chinese people can stand in the aisle of a train? Too many. I can no longer see Heather as three—T-H-R-E-E—people were somehow able to cram between us. Linda and I chatted, while Heather joined the conversation via text messages.

The body heat caused the cabin temperature to rise, and since most people on this train, like me, had not showered for many days, the stench of body odor was overwhelming. The only time air circulated in was when passengers got on and off at each stop. I was near the point of joining the crying baby when we rolled into Zhengzhou and caught a well-running taxi to whisk us home.

After four days with no shower or western toilet, I was never so happy to be back at Sias and the teacher's dorms. I showered, standing there until I ran all the hot water out of my personal heater. I was tempted to let the water reheat and do it again, but that would have been wasteful.

It was fun to reconnect with friends and hear about their home visits. I was glad that I went. I had pushed myself. I saw how a big chunk of the world lives. I met people, tried new foods, and gained a fresh perspective. That would hold me for a while.

CHAPTER 14

LIVING LIKE A ROCK STAR

Standing on the balcony of the ancient monastery overlooking the valley below, it was easy to fall in love with the sights of central China. It was a rare, clear day where the sky was actually blue with scattered, wispy clouds. The terraced landscape below alternated shades of yellow, green, and red as spring brought wildflowers to the ancestral mountain.

For a brief moment, I was not a teacher or an expat, I was transported to a simpler time. Standing there atop Shizu Mountain, I pondered how life had changed so little in thousands of years.

"Teacher, we should have lunch now."

And back to reality.

The dozen students who had organized the hike for me and another teacher, kept us on a tight schedule. Climb to the top: Check. Take pictures and look around: Check. Eat lunch: To do.

As we started our way down out of the monastery, there was a group of four twenty-something Chinese guys sitting near the stairs and playing cards. I was nearly past them when one of the four shouted, "Joey!"

Since this is not my name, I kept walking. Until another voice added: "Time. Machine. Go!"

I stopped.

Seven months earlier, I played "Joey" in the Culture Week skit where my character and The Professor—who had invented a time machine—took a trip through American history.

None of the four young men were my students—they didn't know any of the students with me—but they remembered me from a skit that was on the fringe of my memory. Nearly twelve miles from the university and atop a mountain climbed by thousands, our worlds came together.

They called me back—my Chinese is poor but I do know *guo-lai*, "come here." So there on the balcony of an ancient Buddhist temple on top of a sacred mountain, we raised paper cups full of lukewarm Pepsi to "Joey" and "Time. Machine. Go."

After the final *ganbei*—an American "chug"—my students and I descended the stairs and resumed our schedule. I found myself chuckling unexpectedly throughout lunch as the craziness of the situation sunk into my brain. My students were less than pleased with the actions of the young men and many other Chinese tourists in general.

"The next one who wants a photo with you," Michael said, "we will tell them, *shi kuai* (ten bucks)."

The eleven echoed and agreed with his idea. While I understood their frustration at the near constant interruptions, the idea of charging people money to take a picture with me seemed ludicrous...at the time. Come year two, three, and beyond, I began to understand why celebrities try to avoid the paparazzi.

Being a light-haired, light-eyed foreigner in China is a double-edged sword. It is impossible to blend in anywhere. When I lived in the United States, I could somewhat melt into the background. If I saw people pointing and heard whispers, I could assume they were looking and pointing at someone else and not me, the awkward, overweight girl. However, I couldn't do that in China. One, the locals were not as discreet as mean girls in the States. Two, I was the only person in the direction of their stares and taunts. At first, it really stung, but then it became actually liberating. In the U.S., if I'd voice concerns about whispers, people would say that I was being paranoid. In China, I knew I wasn't paranoid. They said I was fat, and my friends still loved me. They said I was an old maid, and my guy friends still wanted to play volleyball with me. I leaned harder into my community and found acceptance, and the pointing and whispers faded into the background.

The other side of the sword was the overt attention lavished on a person merely for being born in the United States. The number of times I was asked, "Please, make photo you," is staggering. To think of my face being in photos all around China is crazy. But, in all honesty, there's a piece of me that really enjoyed the attention. That little piece of me that grew up in Southern California, that took acting lessons to balance out all those dance classes, and that really wanted to be an actor. *Hi, my name is Kim, I'm a cliché. Hi, Kim.*

The first time it happened it felt absurd that a total stranger wanted a photo with me just because I was a *laowai*. Any foreigner will do really, but then there is the extra excitement when I can tell them, *Wo shi Meiguoren,* "I'm an American." And then all *diyu* breaks loose. People started handing me their babies to take pictures with—granted with all the horror stories I'd read about China, at first, I thought they were *giving* me their children. They pestered their older children to recite various literature passages or western idioms in front of me, anxiously awaiting my approval of their English skills. I gave every kid a massive smile and high five, even if I couldn't understand a thing they said. I was not going to be the "Ugly American" and cause them to lose face.

There were tricky spaces to navigate as well. Chinese friends and students are eager to please, and sometimes without intending to, I've had diva moments. The offhanded comment of "Man, I could drink bubble teas all day to wash away this Xinzheng dust," after I coughed during office hours, led to students overrunning me with drinks in classes the following week as students present in the office hour passed the word to *all* my other classes. Yes, it was very sweet and amazing not to be parched in class, but I also felt like I was taking advantage of their good hearts. On another occasion, I was telling students what a fun time I'd had visiting the nearby city of Kaifeng, which is famous for its peanut cake—think the inside of a Butterfinger candy bar—and old city scrolls that are so long my outstretched arms can't fully extend them. Later in the year, two male students rented bikes for the weekend and rode the one hundred miles round trip to get me peanut cake and a scroll for my parents.

"Are you crazy?" I asked them when they told me what they had done.

"It is not so far, and we stayed with a friend to visit. It was windy, but not so bad."

I was flabbergasted. I have a hard time driving twenty minutes to the mall to pick out a gift, much less cycling for hours. Making it even more special was these two were no longer my students, there was nothing for them to gain by their exploits. They honestly just wanted to do something nice for a friend.

Over time, I learned to phrase things and recall things in such a way as to not start a stampede of gifts. Life on campus became more normal as the students and their families became accustomed to so many foreigners. There were still odd moments away from campus.

I can easily recall my most fearful moment in China. It was not walking down a dark alley after midnight with two friends. It was not learning to surf in choppy Hainan seas. It was not traveling by myself in Beijing. No, my most fearful time in China came when a small group of people turned into a giant swarm that cut me off physically and visually from my friends.

At just over five-feet tall, obstructing my view is not difficult. Over the years, I have adapted to be stealthy and quick on my feet to juke in and out of crowds and catch glimpses of the group I'm with to avoid being lost or left behind. One of our first school cultural trips was to the chrysanthemum festival in Kaifeng. I was walking with Shannon, who, at five-foot-three, is a giant next to me. Despite being sixteen years my junior, Shannon and I bonded at the teacher's camp over our amazing paintball skills.

Meandering through the festival grounds, locals started asking to "make photo" with us. Some people wanted one picture with both of us, others wanted just one of us at a time. It was just a handful of people at first, and then suddenly there was less space around me and, finally, there were people all around me, still jostling me for a photo. I couldn't see Shannon, and my heart started to race. I twisted and turned and wedged my way through the crowd and, finally, caught a glimpse of Shannon. By her wide-eyed expression, she seemed to be feeling the same claustrophobia. We picked and moved our way to each other and together made a compact human crowd-breaker, just like a massive icebreaker in the arctic. Once free of the mass, we could breathe and stretch our limbs.

For me, the biggest rock-star moment came my fourth year. My friend Joe had started a teacher's volleyball team that he generously let me play on despite raising the average age by ten years. In the early stages, we had a large number of foreign teachers and we broke into teams and played against each other.

Slowly, the number of people settled into a smaller group, and we started to play the university's men's volleyball team. It was so much fun. It was a chance to get to know students outside the classroom. One of the most outgoing players was Feng, who quickly became a staple of our conversations and outdoor dining experiences.

We'd been playing games with them for more than a year, when Feng asked if we'd be willing to travel to his hometown and play his former high school's boys' volleyball team. He would make all the arrangements for transportation and lodging at his parent's house, we just had to play. It took him a while to get things together, and I honestly had forgotten when I got the text the van would pick us up later that day.

The van ride to his town was similar to every athletics bus trip I've ever taken, laughing, joking, eating, yelling, singing, and bragging. The similarities stopped when we reached his house. He took us in and introduced us to his family, including his brother who had won numerous awards for his calligraphy. Feng had been living in his brother's shadow for decades. His brother outshined him at school as well. But that was about to change as Feng arrived at his alma mater with a van full of foreign teachers.

When we arrived, we were taken on a mini tour of the school grounds and then led to the boardroom where we met the faculty. We were shown old year books, learned the history of the school's athletics program and given refreshments. The black-top court was flanked by three-story classrooms. When we first started playing, there weren't too many students around. However, as the matches went on, students stood along the balconies and were standing three deep around the court. We played the boys' team and a faculty team several times. We're all pretty convinced they let us win. Afterward, the faculty said they were taking us to dinner and paying for hotel rooms for us for the night. While we were excited by the offer and really wanted to take it, it's still customary in China to say, "No" a few times before relenting.

"We'd like to buy you dinner and pay for your hotel," the superintendent said.

"Oh, thank you, but that is too much, we couldn't."

"You must. We insist. It is our honor."

"No, it would be our honor, but, no, we can't. It's too much."

"Enough crazy talk! Let's go have some dinner, and we'll show you to the hotel."

"Okay. You are the best hosts we have had here in China. Thank you so very much."

We had way too much food. The massive circular table and lazy Susan were overcrowded with all sorts of dishes. I wasn't sure what a lot of things were, so I stuck to what I knew: Mushrooms, *bok choy*, noodles, and fruit.

All the faculty members were enjoying the evening, and judging from the smile on Feng's face, he had been elevated up the social ladder. He was coming out of his brother's shadow, and if it took us playing volleyball and getting free food and lodging in the process, it was well worth it. What good is being a rock star, if you can't sway public opinion of your friends?

What's the hardest thing about being a rock star in China? Leaving China and just being me. It's embarrassing the number of times upon my return to the States when people would ask me to take a photo *for* them that I heard *with* them and tried to get in the picture.

"Wait, what? You don't want to take a photo with me?" My verbal processor giving me away. Thankfully, they always laughed as if I'd made a big joke. But every now and then, when the wind was just right and I caught a Mandarin phrase on the wind, I'd find myself chatting with Chinese visitors in California. I shared where I lived and taught and the famous cities I visited in China. They'll tell me where they'd been in America. I tried to remember any Mandarin to "wow" them. They'd giggle and then act impressed. And when the stars aligned…

"It has been so great to meet you," they'd say.

"It is my pleasure," I say with a fist-clasped nod and slight bow. "I hope America treats you as well as China treated me."

"Yes, yes, and, may we make photo with you?"

Sweet, yelled my inner rock star as I stepped into frame.

CHAPTER 15

WHICH NEWSPAPER IS LYING?

There are few things more enjoyable and nerve-racking than teaching journalism and freedom of the press in a communist country.

It was extra sweet for me because when I was originally hired by the university, it was as an oral English (OE) teacher. The idea of spending hours creating charts on vowel sounds and designing games to help students improve their "th" sound did not seem appealing to me. I was girding myself for the job when I was called into the foreign faculty liaison's office and met David. We clicked right away because he was a former quarterback at Virginia Tech and I was a former college football reporter.

David brought me in to discuss moving from oral English to academics. I wasn't really sure what the move entailed, but it appeared to mean moving away from creative story time, so it was already a more appealing position.

"With your journalism background, we thought you'd be a great fit for the newspaper and magazine class," he said thumbing through papers in a manila folder that I assumed included my résumé. "You may still have to have one or two oral English classes. We're not sure yet."

Less appealing.

"I would love to be able to put my degree to work again. I could probably teach newspapers all week," I said, hoping to avoid double duty.

"We don't have that many classes. You'll have half the classes, and Alan—another former journalist—will have the others."

"Sounds great."

I left the meeting with mixed feelings. I'd been massively relieved at the thought of not teaching oral English, but then teaching an academic and English class seemed worse than just teaching the OE classes.

Later that day, David messaged me to let me know that I'd be a full-time academic teacher. I would teach the newspaper course along with the standard reading course. I found Alan to let him know I was joining his team. While Alan was older than me, he did not come off like the "good-old boy" reporters I worked with at a major Sacramento metro newspaper or the cranky ones in old movies. He hooked me up with the textbook, a softbound collection of various newspaper stories and jargon.

"I teach it more like a current events class," my white-haired teaching partner told me. "I have them come to class ready to share something they found online. Since I randomly call on them, they all come prepared."

"That sounds perfect," I said, noting it meant less lesson planning. "Do you use any of the clips from the book? These are so out of date."

"No, but I do use the front section that goes over newsworthy terms, good to build a shared vocabulary."

"Great. Sounds like it will be easy to stay on the same page."

By the next semester, Alan and I were on different pages.

I kept the current events ice breaker because Alan was right; it really kept the students on their toes not knowing who was going to be called on during that first block of class. I added writing and newspaper comparison.

The majority of Chinese students I knew read English exceptionally well, a strong contingent spoke English well, but it was very difficult to find a solid English writer. My colleagues who taught classes with any type of composition often complained about poor sentence structure and bemoaning the systemic plagiarism problem.

Talking with my students, I learned that copying and pasting full passages without citing sources was perfectly allowed by their Chinese teachers. In addition, their sentence structures were also accepted by their Chinese teachers because they followed Mandarin grammar rules. My students were neither lazy nor belligerent, they were just twentysomethings who were doing what they'd done their entire school careers until some foreigners said it was wrong.

"Okay, I'll make a deal with you that one of my professors made with me," I told every class that first semester. "In this class, you follow my writing rules, and I guarantee you'll pass. Starting today, all of you have As—100% grades—and it's up to you to do the work to stay there."

When I was given this option as a college student I liked it, so I took it for my students. The idea of starting at 100% and possibly slipping was a thousand times better than starting at zero and trying to build up from there. The idea resonated with my students, who were grade driven. They were still skeptical of my writing rules but were willing to give them a shot. The first thing was to learn how to paraphrase. They'd been inadvertently doing it with their current events as they retold the news each class. But now it was time to make it more of a formal exercise.

They would be given a series of basic sentences:

There was a fire on Monday.

The ancient capital building burned to the ground.
A kitten was found safe.
Seven firemen were hurt putting out a fire in Kaifeng.
The police arrested a man suspected of setting a temple on fire.

From the sentences, they pulled out the who/what/where/when/why/how and used them as building blocks to write their news stories. The first time I used this lesson the results were comical.

Monday a kitten was safe after a fire burned down Kaifeng's capital building.

On Monday, firemen saved a kitten from a fire in Kaifeng.

All of their work started with the time element and focused on the kitten. Not one of them mentioned that firemen had been hurt or that a man was arrested. Starting with the time element followed standard Chinese sentence structure, but I wasn't sure how to convince them that kittens weren't the most important detail.

"Your first sentences were very interesting. Let's try again with some new rules. For news stories, people come before animals, especially wounded people and safe animals. Also, if there is a crime, that would be written about before safe animals."

Some of them nodded their heads in comprehension, a few girls shook their heads and got misty eyed, as if I'd just kicked the kitty. Their next attempts were much better, but had a hint of annoyance with me and my rules.

The police arrested a man for burning down an ancient capital building in Kaifeng on Monday. There were many firemen hurt. The kitten was safe. Do not worry about the kitten.

That student kept her "A" that week.

As their reading and writing skills improved, I added a lesson on critical thinking. Western schools implement the idea early, and students are often asked to ponder and reach their own conclusions. This is a polar opposite style to the Eastern discipline of rote memorization. Chinese students are not asked to draw their own conclusions. Their way of thinking is determined for them, and I had numerous exchanges with them.

"Teacher, what is the meaning of this?"

"The writer is leaving that up to you. What do you think the point of the article is?"

"What do you think?"

"My opinion doesn't matter. For this exercise, I want to know what you think."

"How should I think?"

"Ha, I can't tell you that. You can say how you feel. You can't lose points for your opinion."

"Okay. I will try."

I learned that when I became weary of the circular arguments, I just had to tell them they couldn't lose points for having an opinion, and that usually satisfied them.

To tie this lesson into their news value vocabulary—proximity, prominence, timeliness, etc.—I had them track a story through "Today's Front Pages" on the Newseum website. (Easily one of the coolest and geekiest journalism tools.) The website features the front pages of most major metropolitan newspapers from around the world. It is a great way to see how news values impact the way newspapers design their front page.

Students had to pick two newspapers from different columns. I had papers divided by liberal versus conservative and East coast versus West coast. Most students picked *The New York Times* versus *The Los Angeles Times*; a few took *The Sacramento Bee* (pretty sure it was a kiss-up move) and *The New York Times*. Once they had their papers, they were assigned to track a topic for the remainder of the semester. These topics ranged from conservation, water and global warming, to politics and, if it was an election year, a specific candidate.

As an academic teacher, I was lucky enough to be assigned to classrooms with audio-visual equipment. I could post side-by-side images of newspapers and talk about how putting a bolder headline on a story and placing it near the top indicated that the newspaper felt that was more important than the smaller story with the lighter type face at the bottom. I'd also point out the use of photography—a photo's size, placement, and cropping could sometimes say more than a thousand words. To shake things up, on days when there was a major international story, I'd also bring up the front page of *China Daily* and other Asian newspapers.

This lesson, while fun, was also riddled with trouble for me. Most newspapers had similar story placement for global warming and conservation stories, but a paper's bias showed on the political front. Conservative-leaning papers tended to highlight Republicans and their causes in a good light, and liberal-leaning papers shone a spotlight on the good works of Democrats. On the flipside, these papers tended to make the opposition look bad or ignored them altogether. Any time I saw a major political squabble pop up on the Internet, I knew the next newspaper class would be interesting.

"Which of these papers is lying?" asked one of my top students as she slammed the eleven-by-seventeen-inch sheets of paper on my desk. The *thwap* surprised even her. "I am sorry, Teacher." She ducked her head and fumbled trying to straighten the papers. "Please, Teacher, which paper is lying?" she said in a controlled voice, once again head high.

"Neither is lying..."

"One must be! See?!" She shoved the papers toward me. "In this one, the man's face is angry, and the story says he is angry.

But...but in this one," she rearranged the pages and pointed to President Barack Obama's face. "In this one, he is happy, and the story says he is happy. He cannot be angry and happy about the same thing. Which is lying?"

I was ecstatic for her gusto. I was annoyed at the two newspapers for making my job tough that day. "Technically, neither is lying. They are picking and choosing which parts of his plan to write about and selecting a photo to emphasize their choice. This paper wants to highlight that he has trouble with the legislature, while this one is focusing on the few items he was able to move forward. Does that make sense?"

"No. One must not be telling the truth."

I waited to see if she was going to add anything else, but she just stood there staring at me, waiting for me to explain it better.

"They are both telling the slice of truth that they feel their readers want to know about. No one newspaper tells everything. It's important with U.S. newspapers to read several and then use your critical thinking skills."

"That is stupid," she said shaking her head. At that moment, I couldn't argue the point. "In China, I pick up *China Daily*, and it says, 'This is so.' I pick up the Zhengzhou newspaper, and it also says, 'This is so.' I hear the news on TV or radio, and they also say, 'This is so.' They all say the same exact thing, and *that* is how I know it is truth."

I let the weight of her words and its implication settle on my thoughts. There was no dissenting voice in the Chinese media. I took a breath.

"Wow, for an American, *that* is crazy," I said. "If Americans woke up tomorrow and the *L.A. Times* and *New York Times* and CNN and Fox News were all saying the exact same thing, they would swear someone had taken over the press. The fact that they're all different lets us know they have freedom to print their stories and opinions."

"That is crazy, Teacher."

I could see her point that having one consistent news source provided a sense of reassurance and the idea of truth, but as a journalist, the idea of a media controlled by the government brought me no assurance of truth or peace.

The title of the course was "Newspaper and Magazine Reading," so twice a semester, I hauled in a box laden with the latest magazines mailed to me from friends and family in the U.S.: *People, U.S. News and World Report, The Economist, National Geographic, Sports Illustrated, Time, Better Homes and Gardens,* etc. Students loved flipping through the magazines because of all the photographs. They were less impressed with the in-depth articles that featured "too many new words."

For this assignment, I placed the magazines at stations around the room and had the students divide into groups of three or four. They would rotate through the stations, answering questions about the set of magazines: What is the focus of this magazine? Who would you recommend read this magazine? What are the best and worst parts of this magazine? I walked around the classroom to make sure they were talking in English and filling out their papers.

I typically reviewed all the new magazines to make sure there was no offensive copy that could get me in trouble. However, this time I hadn't. I thought, *Why should I check? Every other magazine has been perfectly fine. What could go wrong?*

Those words tumbled back through my mind as I walked toward the group with a series of *National Geographic* magazines. Even though it was upside down to me, one of the photos caught my eye. There was a slight, white-clad figure in front of large brownish shapes. As I approached and tilted my head to see it right-side up, I was staring at the iconic Tank Man photograph taken by Jeff Widener of the Associated Press. The photo of the lone individual, holding his grocery bags and standing in front of four Chinese tanks was one of the most seen following the 1989 Tiananmen Square massacre. The Chinese government denied the "incident" happened. A cold tingle crept up my spine, and I expected elite forces to break into my classroom at any moment. No one busted down my door, however, and I left the magazine with the others. I figured more than half the class had seen it already, to take it away now I thought would draw suspicion. When I read through the student's papers later that night, not one of them mentioned Tiananmen in their *National Geographic* reviews. Since it wasn't circulating in Chinese news, I wondered if they just passed it off as U.S. propaganda.

I was feeling pretty good about the progress my students were making on their writing in my class, but I was still hearing from a number of other academic teachers that plagiarism was alive and well. I wasn't naïve enough to think that I could change the entire system with one newspaper class, but I was cocky enough to try to change the habit of the students I had each semester.

The crux for my students—and I assume other Chinese students—was that until they had Western teachers they had not run into the idea of plagiarism. When foreign teachers had encountered the problem, they did what professors in the United States would do and failed the paper. This ignited a major firestorm in my first semester as students brought grievances galore to the administration. There were numerous meetings where the Western staff explained how literally printing a page from the Internet—the student didn't even copy and paste onto a word document—was not a completed work assignment. The administration did what it always did in these situations: The student redid the assignment, and turned it into a Chinese faculty member for grading, with the caveat the student could score no higher than seventy percent.

I asked several of my students-turned-friends why they thought our educational cultures seemed to differ so much on this topic. The first point was always, "We've never been taught that before." I'd heard it so many times before, and I was hoping to move beyond that dead horse.

"What *were* you taught?" And that opened floodgates of information.

Early Chinese education for my students included long hours spent with rote memorization. I can remember as a kid memorizing the alphabet, numbers to one hundred and easy addition. My brain still hurts when I recall learning various multiplication tables and grammar rules. Thank goodness for *Schoolhouse Rock*, or I'm not sure I'd have remembered conjunctions and their functions or interjections and their expressions.

However, for my students, it went beyond letters and numbers. Woven throughout their education were nationwide tests that determine a student's place in the educational system. Elementary students were given several paragraphs of the writings by Chairman Mao to memorize. They were later given a test on these paragraphs and graded on how precisely they reproduced the original copy. One of my friends said he would spend hours memorizing and then writing and rewriting. His parents would look it over for him and if just one character was off—for example in English writing "a" instead of "an"—he was sent back to do it all over again. During this process, no teacher ever said, "Oh, by the way, remember to cite your source and start your paper with, 'According the writings of Mao Zedong.'"

Because of this way of learning and doing, whenever a teacher explained plagiarism as not doing the work, students would respond, "But I did do the work." And for them and their educational background, they had. They found the articles. They memorized the articles. They wrote them from memory. There was no getting around their logic, and, since there was no support from the Chinese faculty, Western teachers cracked down on obvious downloads. "At least copy and paste it into another document to show 'extra' effort."

Teaching a newspaper class gave me a reason to actually teach a section on plagiarism. During my fifteen years of sports writing and editing, I'd seen several reporters lose their jobs because they were tired or got lazy and copied someone else's work. It hit extra close to home when a reporter from the neighboring town's paper lifted several paragraphs from a story in our sports section when I was the editor. He was able to keep his job, but he lost the respect of our staff. I felt if I could make it personal, then maybe, just maybe, my students would at least be less likely to use someone else's words as their own.

Without using names, I put the stories on the screen side-by-side. The plagiarized sections were highlighted. Students were asked to read one section then the other to see if there was a difference. No, they all agreed they were the same words and same sentence structure.

"Do you see how this is plagiarism? He stole someone's work." There was no reaction. "What if it was your work?"

"I would not have a trouble with that," one of my students volunteered and many others nodded in agreement, some even verbalized their agreement.

"What if I told you, he stole my friend's work?"

There were murmurings around the room and exchanged glances. Again, teachers have a place of honor in the Chinese system, so stealing from a teacher or their friend was not acceptable and from me, a teacher they knew, even less acceptable.

"Do you know his excuse?" All of them shook their heads. "He said that he had been working on the same story, that he read our story first, and then became distracted with something else. He said it was really late by the time he got back to the story, that he was tired and not thinking straight. He said he thought he wrote his own story and didn't even remember reading our story until we called to inquire about it."

I was surprised at how riled I was at remembering the incident. It wasn't just that he had stolen something, my anger was because we'd known each other for more than a decade. It hurt personally *and* professionally.

"It's important for me as your teacher that you understand how important this is," I said, pausing and regrouping. "Some of you want to go to America and continue your education. Plagiarism can get you expelled. Not a do-over and a 'C' grade. Expelled. Done. Out. If you do your best, if you don't get lazy, if you don't wait until the last minute, if you just cite your source, you'll be okay. Can you all remember to cite your sources?"

A chorus of "Yes" echoed around the room. They stuck to it...in my class, at least. Granted, over the five years I was there, I couldn't convince them not to cheat on their multiple choice exams, but that's another story.

CHAPTER 16

PLAY. PAUSE. REPEAT.

It's hard to think of a more sought after job that watching movies all day. In my second year at Sias, I was tapped to be one of the lucky few.

The previous year, Andrei did all the hard work of developing a new curriculum. The university had an *American Culture Through Film* textbook that contained numerous old movies that U.S. film majors weren't even forced to watch. Andrei, a film and television writing and acting master, curated a list of films that were useful for showing Western thought, while still being highly entertaining and relevant to the students. The one movie that survived the textbook purge was *Guess Who's Coming to Dinner*, a classic that holds up and teaches values that never go out of style.

Andrei used a different movie every other week to not only discuss culture but also to delve into film structure. Students learned about a plot, climax, genre, theme, and symbolism, to name a few. This exposure and knowledge gave them a skill set to break down films and engage others in conversation. With limited English, students often talked about beautiful weather and delicious food. Now, they had an expanded vocabulary and could work on engaging in thematic conversations.

Classes saw on average five movies a semester. Certain films were shown each semester, including *Back to the Future*, *The Truman Show*, and *Guess Who's Coming to Dinner*. Other movies that were rotated through (depending on my mood) were *The Wizard of Oz*, *The Phantom of the Opera* (2004), *The Prince of Egypt*, *October Sky*, *Casablanca*, *Raiders of the Lost Ark*, and *The Princess Bride*.

The format consisted of watching a movie in one class then discussing it during the next class with the addition of a new term. This style culminated with the final project, where students were placed in groups, assigned a new movie to watch and then create a PowerPoint lesson like the ones I had made for each film we watched. They would stand and deliver the presentation to their classmates. Finals typically took at least two full class periods because my students—who had trouble answering a question in their seats—loved to stand up and perform.

I enjoyed this class for the freedom it gave me as a teacher, and for the way it allowed me to see a different side of my students, and, ironically, learn more about Chinese culture in the process. There is something about art—film, painting, writing, sculpture—that allows people to make a deeper connection on topics that they typically may avoid. My theory on this is that there are some charged topics that people try to avoid, or when they do talk about them with someone else their automatic defenses emerge. However, if two people are looking at a painting that deals with a charged subject matter, the art acts as a buffer when they talk about it. They're no longer coming at each other directly, but instead reacting to the piece, putting the artist's ideals—and not their own—in the crosshairs.

The movies shown in class were more about human connection and emotion than political statements, although *Guess Who's Coming to Dinner* allowed for discussions on race relations and cultural differences, and *Raiders of the Lost Ark* gave students the opportunity to look at the power of political and religious symbols.

The downside of teaching a film class was watching a movie three to five times a week, which is why I changed up some of the original films taught in the class. After back-to-back classes of *The Wizard of Oz*, I was ready to get everyone and their little dogs, too. Even *The Truman Show* had me nodding off after the third viewing. Why didn't I just leave the room and let the class go on without me? That would have been against the university rules.

First-time viewings for students always entertained me. I nearly fell out of my seat laughing as the women and men screamed and squirmed during the Egyptian tomb scene in *Raiders*, when Indy and Marion broke through the wall and encountered thousands of snakes and skeletons. "Teacher, why are you having us watch a horror film?" screamed several students as they covered their eyes. I laughed again and assured them this was not a horror film. I'm not sure they all believed me.

Another favorite for the students was *The Princess Bride*. While my fellow teachers also enjoyed the movie, they were less fond of me after I showed it.

"Hey, Kim, you showed *Princess Bride* this week, huh," a teacher told me more than asked.

"Yeah, how did you know?"

"Because all of my students are answering my requests for them to do something with 'As you wish.'"

"Inconceivable!"

"You're not helping."

(In hindsight, it really is lucky that I maintained friendships from those semesters.)

With the majority of my students having seen *Gone with the Wind* and saying how much they loved it—I have to be honest, I'm not a fan—I was certain they would love *The Phantom of the Opera*. The 2004 musical did not let me down. The women loved it because it was full of love and drama and music, and the men loved it because Gerard Butler—aka Leonidas of *300*—was the *Phantom*. It also allowed us to look at how something like the color red, a very good luck color in China, can be seen as love or hate in Western films. When Christine walked through the cemetery and saw a glowing red crypt, my students were convinced this meant all was well, and she could enter the crypt. They were surprised when I told them that in this case it meant danger, and that she should instead run away. This film always received positive feedback, but I later learned they liked it because it was so long it took up nearly two class sessions.

The one movie that touched them the most was *October Sky*. It's not a flashy film with catchy one-liners or staggering musical scores, instead, it's a film that comes closest to matching their own lives, and they were able to relate to Homer Hickam. They understood what it was like to live in a community dependent on coal. Xinzheng and Coalwood, West Virginia, are on opposite sides of the world, but they are connected by coal production. Solidifying the connection, Homer was at odds with his father over what he wanted to do when he grew up. The vast majority of my students—especially the women who were expected to be married by the time they were twenty-four—had (or were avoiding) similar discussions with their parents. Usually, there was a lot of whispering during the movies, but all the classes dialed in to this film. I was overwhelmed the first time I showed this film and heard students sniffling and saw them wiping away tears as Homer's dad arrived for the final rocket launch. I fought back my own tears at seeing male students with watery eyes.

I was hoping that same emotion would carry over for *Guess Who's Coming to Dinner*. My students were not as excited for a film made in 1967, so I had to up the ante and create a reason for them to engage. They knew the film was about racial discrimination, but I added the Hollywood backstory of Katherine Hepburn and Spencer Tracy's love story, how Tracy was dying and this would be his last film. Now, I had them hooked. They enjoyed the movie. They laughed at the right times, and booed the bigot at the right times. While Spencer Tracy's character came around at the end, I had to explain that many Americans remained prejudiced, and interracial couples were still harassed. My students found this horrible—as they should—and insisted their parents would not care if they came home with a Black boyfriend or girlfriend. And knowing how some parents hope their children will marry foreigners, I can't argue with them. But I did have one ace up my sleeve that I played sparingly, and only with classes that I knew very well.

"Your parents wouldn't mind you dating a foreigner of any color?"

Heads shake and some add a verbal, "No."

"They would just be happy if you're happy?"

Nodding heads across the room.

Should I really ask this next question? I am just doing it to feel better about my own country's shortcomings? Possibly. Probably.

"What if you wanted to date a Japanese person?"

All eyes fixed on me. I hit an exposed nerve. The animosity that bordered on hate that exists between China and Japan goes back eons. China suffered terribly under Japan during World War II. The destruction of the city of Nanjing is immortalized in movies and books. There is a contest every year to honor the best new artworks dealing with the massacre that left between 50,000 and 300,000 dead, depending on the source. Once, a student asked me in class, "You, too, hate the Japanese for what they did at Pearl Harbor?" I paused to collect my thoughts. "No,

I don't hate the Japanese. My grandpa fought in the Pacific, so I don't have any love for them either. But, as a country, we dropped two bombs on them, so that kind of put us ahead." The Chinese people didn't have their moment of retribution.

Ironically, one of the foreign languages that students can take at the university was Japanese, taught by native Japanese, and there were Japanese students in the international program. My students were in that weird place of growing up being told a group of people are evil but then actually meeting some of *those* people and realizing they actually like them.

But how *much* did they like them? Could a couple of years in a university undo centuries of belief? After a very long pause—that gave me plenty of time to regret asking—my students were a mixed bunch. Some sat rigid, lips thin, arms crossed. Others were shaking and then nodding their heads.

"Yes, if he were American-Japanese." Most of the class agreed this was a good compromise that their parents would also agree with. It was clear both of our countries had far to go with race relations.

The movie that effected my students and me the most was the 2009 short film *The Butterfly Circus*. My first introduction to it was when Andrei sent me a copy to help edit the subtitles from Spanish to English. I soon found myself not typing and just watching the film. In twenty minutes, director and writer Joshua Weigel had me smiling, weeping, and cheering the redemption story. I'd watched numerous three-hour-plus long epics that dealt with acceptance and community and unconditional love, but they paled in comparison to the impact of this film. I wondered how I was going to be able to handle my emotions in class. I couldn't teach a lesson and blubber at the same time. I prayed for strength to teach the lesson.

The film followed Will, played by Nick Vujicic, a limbless man who lived in a circus sideshow, where he is accosted with hateful speech and rotten fruit. He encountered Mr. Mendez (Eduardo Verástegui), who was the ringmaster of the Butterfly Circus that features people who have been abused by the world but found hope and family with each other. Will's transformation is heartbreaking and triumphant. Similar to *October Sky*, my students were transfixed and emotionally impacted by this film. *The Butterfly Circus* tapped into the part of a person's brain that says "You're not good enough," "You're too different," "You're broken," and instead instills the anthem, "All are welcome in this family. Come be healed. Come be held. Come be loved." Like a favorite book, every now and then, I take twenty minutes to watch the film and refresh my weary soul.

There is something about a really great story that you can watch or read over and over and never get tired of it, which is really helpful when you know you're going to play and repeat five more times.

CHAPTER 17

LESSONS FOR TEACHER

While I loved teaching, a big part of my reasoning to move to China was to learn. I gained a deeper spiritual understanding through my community, and through my Chinese students, I learned more about their culture and myself in the process.

I think the first big lesson for any foreigner is the art of Chinese cooking. The Six Pack showed me around the city on bicycles during the day, and then came to my apartment to teach me how to make dumplings at night. Ironically, the guys did most of the cooking.

"My mother taught me to make dumplings when I was very young," Julian said. "It's very important to roll them correctly and to seal them tightly."

Julian, Michael, and Kevin worked feverishly to pack just the right amount of pork filling in to each dumpling. Julian worked the mini rolling pin—it was slightly larger than the span of his palm—with such deftness that it took him just three rolls to have the dough flat and round. His mother would have been proud. I tried to roll a few myself, and I'm not sure what shape I created. One looked something like Ohio and the other an elephant.

"Maybe you should try to stuff them." I was told and gently sent to the other side of the table. I watched the duo take a pinch of meat, plop it in the middle, pull the dough over and then pull and pinch to give it a classic dumpling seal. I used the teaspoon to scoop out the filling, plopped in the middle, pulled the dough and tried to cinch the edge. It looked more like crinkled crepe paper.

"That would be okay for a wonton."

I loved how whenever I messed up in front of my students that they did their best to find a silver lining for me. They never wanted me to lose face. It was so different than some of my American friendships. I am known for being quite sarcastic, and I've cut a friend down mercilessly with my one-liners. They do the same to me, and we know it's all in fun, but it's very different than having people only trying to lift you up. I'm still sarcastic, but I'm much more aware of my friends who do not like sarcasm and try to limit my use in front of them.

The dinner was amazing. We ate family style with a plate piled high with dumplings in the middle of the table and a small plate and chopsticks in front of each of us. My students were all relieved to learn that I was adept at using *kuaizi* (chopsticks). "You will not starve." They took turns telling me about their hometowns and how they became friends. I learned that they were very much like my college friends and me, full of hopes and dreams, and scared of living up to expectations and letting their villages down.

At times, I've said, "I don't want to let everyone down," fully aware that I didn't know everyone, and most of the ones I did know didn't really care. But for many of my students, they actually had the hopes and dreams and expectations of an entire village on their shoulders. Attending university is expensive, and one like Sias, even more so. Townspeople would pool their resources to send a student to school, with the expectation that they would either return to help or they would send money from wherever they ended up.

One student shared the pressure of being the second-born male of the family. With China's one-child policy firmly in place, his father was informed by the company supervisor that if he kept the child that he would be demoted, his pay would be slashed, and he would never have a chance for advancement. We were all thankful that his parents chose to keep him so he could grow to be our friend, but I could see he carried a heavy burden of wanting to succeed to make their sacrifice worthwhile. As an adopted child, I could relate to the feelings of obligation of thankfulness at being given a shot at life; but I had no point of reference for growing up with the knowledge that your parents had willingly given up so much. I'm sure the story was repeated all across China, and even more so with only children who carried everything on their shoulders.

On one gorgeous day, a group of students wanted to take me to Huangdi's hometown, which is a cultural center dedicated to Huangdi—the Yellow Emperor. He's a cultural hero credited with creating pretty much everything, reading, writing, agriculture, etc. The center in his honor features a river that spans the history of the Middle Kingdom. As we walked by the river, which follows a marble path, my students would stop and read the writing etched into the shiny surface. It noted the various reigns of leaders. We stopped at one that contained the characters for *Meiguo*.

"Ha, this one is about America." I said as proud as a kindergartner who's read a new word.

"Yes, it tells of when your President Nixon visited here."

"Really? Cool."

The river ended up at the front of a building that was flanked by two giant gold dragons.

"Teacher, take your photo with a dragon."

It was not unusual for them to ask me to pose with various landmarks and statues for photos. I walked up the grassy knoll and stood next to the mythical beast—that I could now see was made from Styrofoam. They took their photos and suddenly paled.

"Teacher, teacher, come here quickly," they yelled in unison with arms waving. I wasn't sure what was happening but it seemed very urgent. "Teacher, we just noticed the sign," one said pointing to a six-by-six plaque in the grass. "It says to stay off the grass. You could have been in trouble."

"Me? *You* told me to go out there."

"Oh, my, yes. We are in trouble."

"No one is in trouble," I tried to assure them. "If anyone says anything, I will say it was my idea. Okay?"

They all nodded. They moved a little slower afterward; I think they wanted to make sure they read every sign to avoid potential troubles. The interior of the building was covered in amazing murals that showed all the positive things Huangdi did for China. On the far wall, there was a stunning painting of a dragon in flight over a village. It was the first time it dawned on me that Chinese dragons didn't have massive wings like dragons in European stories.

"Hey, that dragon doesn't have wings." I felt it was my duty to point out the obvious.

"It does not."

"How does it fly?"

With the most serious face I'd seen on a student, she said, "It is a dragon." And then turned away as if that is all I needed to know. Apparently, a dragon, by definition, flies. *Noted.*

We capped off our visit to the old town with a stop in a silk shop. There was a container in the middle of the store full of silk worms and their cocoons. It was interesting and creepy with all the crawly bugs. I did take advantage of the situation and pick up several silk ties and scarves for less than $3 each. It seems as if every time I visited some Chinese cultural spot, I had to buy something. A very East meets West moment every time.

Julian and Michael took it upon themselves to make sure I had a well-rounded cultural experience. Aside from cooking, they introduced me to classic Chinese literature. The Big Three were *A Dream in Red Mansions, Outlaws of the Marsh,* and *Romance of the Three Kingdoms.* They had all been translated numerous times, but Julian wanted to make sure I had the best translation to ensure the easiest reading. *A Dream in Red Mansions* had a similar feel to *The Secret Garden,* as there were special children and loads of family running hither and yon, and no one really seemed to know what was going on until the end.

Far and away my top choice was *Outlaws of the Marsh.* This epic tale of misfits not only entertained me, but it also gave me insight into the Chinese writing style. It was extremely circular in its plot points, which was annoying at first to me, a linear reader. However, once I gave over to it and just got into the story, it was some of the most fantastical writing I've read since Paul Bunyan and his blue Ox. In *Outlaws,* one wayward hero gets drunk out of his head and boxes a tiger and wins.

I knew I was in trouble when I started reading *Romance of the Three Kingdoms.* The main characters were Liu Bei, Cao Cao, and Sun Quan, and they ruled over Shu, Wei, and Wu. Three pages into the story, and I couldn't remember what names went with people and what names went with places. I felt bad when I told Julian that I just couldn't read it and understand it. He was patient and understood. After all, he'd just finished *The Red Badge of Courage* and *Tom Sawyer*, both filled with broken English quotes. He was trying to figure out phrases like, "Th'army's goin' t' move."

"What does it mean?"

"He's saying, 'The army's going to move,' but the writer is trying to give you a feel for his dialect. You know how people from Beijing sound different than Shanghai or Chungdu?"

He tilted his head a bit, but then gave it a good shake.

"Okay, let's try this. Don't think about the words. Just say out loud what you see really fast. Try to hear it more than read it."

"Tharmies goint move."

"Close, try a bit slower."

"Thu army's gonna move."

"Great."

"I get it. I will read the dialogue out loud in the future."

Michael went a different route. He introduced me to Chinese poetry. He brought me a small book with paintings of birds on the front. The poems were in Chinese and English, and he read some of his favorites to me. They all painted very vivid pictures of nature and man's place in it. I shared with him my collection of Robert Frost poems, which he fell in love with. Since I couldn't find another copy in China, I let Michael keep the book.

In addition to catching up on literature, I tried watching some of my students' favorite movies. I was a horrible student of Chinese films. I didn't have trouble with subtitles, but I stumbled following some plots because I didn't know the cultural backstory or meaning of certain gestures. When we were watching *The Truman Show*, students learned about crossing fingers to cover up telling a lie when they see the close up of Truman's wife's hands in the wedding photo. They were unaware of the gesture, but the majority of Western viewers would know right away it meant she was actually lying.

"I thought it meant good luck," several students chimed in at once.

"It does when you show it and say it," I said, and then put my hands behind my back. "But when you cross them behind your back or hide them in some way, it's meant to allow you to get away with a lie."

"That's weird."

"Yes, yes, it is. And you thought English language was hard."

If I stuck to classic Chinese action films, I didn't really have to worry about subplots. The movie *Red Cliff* remained one of my favorite, and included my old friend Cao Cao from *The Three Kingdom's* novel. This is a pretty straight forward war movie and, in my opinion, on par with *Tora, Tora, Tora* or *Midway* (1976). There was strategy and betrayal and loads of battle scenes.

The one movie that was nearly mandatory for all Chinese to watch was *The Monkey King*, which was a retelling of the book *The Journey to the West*. The movie has been made and remade several times and was shown at every Spring Festival. It's like *The Ten Commandments* at Easter or *The Sound of Music* at Christmas. The Monkey King was a trickster who eventually became enlightened by a monk. There was also a giant pig involved. I'd seen bits of it here and there, but I have not been able to sit all the way through it. It feels like a children's show from my youth where people lived with giant puppets. There was a nostalgia to it, but since I didn't grow up with it, I just couldn't connect to it. It would be like seeing *The Sandlot* as a kid and falling in love with it, but later in life when showing it to friends who had never seen it, they would find it silly and dated.

It was also interesting for me to find out what my students thought of Western movies' depictions of Chinese people and culture. In 2008, two movies hit China—one to acclaim, the other to flames. *Kung Fu Panda* was easily one of my classes' favorite films that semester. They loved that the wise tortoise was named Oogway. "His name means tortoise." And that Tigress, Mantis, Crane, Viper, and Monkey were all actual forms of *kung fu.*

"What parts of this movie do you think they got right about China, and what parts are wrong?"

"Well, Teacher, as you know, China is famous for the *gung fu,*" started a student using the traditional name for the martial art. "And China is also famous for the pandas. However, the panda does not do the *gung fu.*"

It took all my effort not to laugh, so I nodded my approval with an ever-growing smile on my face. I've used the phrase myself a few times when people ask me what was one of the surprising things about China. "The panda does not do the *gung fu.*" People looked at me like I'm crazy, bordering on super wise.

Easily the top rotten egg of the year—which was not shown in class—was *The Mummy: Tomb of the Dragon Emperor.* The movie had plenty of star power that included Jet Li, but even the actors couldn't save it. My students were upset about the portrayal of Chinese people, the overall ludicrous plot that mixed several traditions and ruined them all. Talking with some of them separately after class, there was a genuine sense of hurt and anger that their culture was being twisted to make the Western characters look better, stronger, and smarter.

Hollywood redeemed itself in 2010 with the release of *The Karate Kid,* staring Jackie Chan and Jaden Smith. My students were more than willing to overlook that karate was not *kung fu* because "the karate comes *from* the *gung fu.*" Putting the movie over the top was Justin Bieber's, "Never Say Never" theme song. Several students picked this version of *The Karate Kid* for their final report. After that week, I was happy to never, no, never hear that song again.

CHAPTER 18

A TIME TO MOURN

There is a drawn out joke for explaining how people should be told about death.

It starts out with a man returning home from vacation where he meets his brother who was housesitting, which included taking care of his cat.

"Welcome home, brother."

"Oh, it's good to be home. Where is my cat?"

"It's dead."

"What?" The brother is obviously distraught and upset at the death of his cat. "What? You can't just say that to someone."

"What would you have liked me to do," his poor excuse of a cat-sitter brother asked.

"You should ease into the bad news gently. Start with, 'Hey, your cat jumped on the roof. I tried to get it down, but there was an accident, and it fell and died.' That's a much better way."

"Okay, I understand."

"Good. So how were Mom and Dad and Grandma while I was away?"

"Well, Grandma jumped onto the roof…"

It usually gets a few chuckles, but does bring up a good point that the way you learn about someone's passing is important.

Growing up around fairly healthy people, I don't remember learning anyone died until I was a sophomore in high school. My great grandma was somewhat of a legend on my mom's side of the family. She'd lived a rough life by today's standards, had loads of kids, fought and beat cancer once, but not the second time. My encounters with her as a young child were a bit frightening. She was gruff and set in her ways, and her house had a smell that I just assumed came from old people. I was sad when I learned she died, but she was eighty-six years old, so it seemed to me she'd had a good long life.

As I got older, sadly, people I knew and felt close to died. It was heartbreaking, and I remember being so thankful for my family and friends at those times. They held me, cried with me, and shared stories about the recently departed. I remember thinking, *I don't know how I'd get through this without my family.* I would soon learn.

My first semester in China, I was in spring break mode. Sure I had a job and things to do, but I was in a new country and having the time of my life. I kept in touch with friends and family through email and Skype. (I had not yet joined social media.) Our correspondences were full of the latest gossip, weather, and I miss yous.

One morning, I saw an email from a dear friend with a generic subject line. I clicked it open expecting to read about their latest picnic on the beach or government conspiracy. Instead, I stood rooted to the floor, the pounding of my heartbeat in my ears the only sound. I read the first line again.

Did you hear J died?

Who the freak starts an email like that!? I had not heard and this was not the way I wanted to hear. I emailed this friend back to get more information. The more I learned the more my heart broke. I sat at my desk, staring at the laptop display. I replayed as many moments that I could remember with my recently departed friend and his family. The fact that he—someone younger than me—was gone was unimaginable. The rest of the day was a a blur. I went to my classes to teach, but headed straight back to my room after each session. I emailed all my friends who also knew him to try to get more information, to try to make a connection, to try to find a way to grieve.

There was a knock at my door.

"Hey, Kim O, you in there?"

I recognized Ruth's voice. Part of me wanted to talk to her, and part of me wanted to wallow. I forced myself out of my chair, shuffled through the hall, and opened the door.

"You weren't at dinner. I wanted to make sure you're okay."

I'm not sure if I burst into tears or wrapped her in a hug first. She hugged me back and led me into my living room.

"What's wrong?" She asked as she got me to the couch. Other friends walked by and she waved them inside. I looked around and saw I was no longer alone. Dear friends sat on the couch or near me on the floor. No one spoke. They all were just there for me. They waited for me to gather myself enough to tell them what was wrong.

As I spoke of J's death, all the hurt and pain came back, but this time I was met by hugs and gentle arm strokes. One friend made some tea. They started to ask questions about my friend, things they did that made me laugh, and craziest things they ever did or said. They didn't know my friend, but they knew me and they did their best to help me through the grieving process. I felt safe and loved with them. I had always thought that they would be there for me, but it was a blessed moment to actually experience that feeling of community from them.

Sadly, the following semester, I was able to comfort others with the comfort I had been given. In April of 2007, twenty-six students and five faculty members were gunned down on the Virginia Tech campus, the alma mater of my friends, Ruth and David. Ruth, a recent graduate, was just a year removed from walking the halls of the buildings where students were murdered. David and Ruth were familiar with the faculty members.

This time we were huddled in Ruth's room on her couch as she processed this horrible event. We held special times of prayer to coincide with vigils being held in Blacksburg, Virginia. We were our own island of support on the far side of the world.

It made me a bit skittish on campus for a few days. Guns are rare in China, the special police have them, but I'd read and heard of numerous knife attacks around the country. Individuals had attacked school children, co-workers, and strangers. It was all so random and added to the overall despair of the time. I honestly don't know how I would have gotten through it without my friends. Having such a strong community helped pull me up and into a place of light where I walked around grateful for each day, for each person, and for each memory.

CHAPTER 19

2008: PARENTS, EARTHQUAKES, AND STINKY TOFU

The number eight is considered a "good luck" number in China. That's why the nation wanted to host the Olympics beginning on August 8th, 2008, the eighth day of the eighth month of the 2008th year. It's a *really* lucky number.

Four is considered the number of bad luck, so it seemed my parents coming to visit in the fifth month of 2008 should be without trouble. But just to be sure, I prayed like I'd never prayed before in my life...including the time my dog was hit by a car.

Living in China had mellowed the dogma of what it meant to be part of a church, but it had amped up my need and desire for prayer. Community requires communication, so how could I commune with God if I didn't talk with Him? When done right, prayer was not some drudgery but a dialogue—I use words, my heavenly Papa uses impressions (sometimes words through other people).

My typical prayers were about health, safety, growth, understanding, and peace for me and others. When my parents told me they had decided to visit me, my prayers became very specific and extra earnest.

Dear God, please, allow the flight to be smooth. May they encounter an English speaker if needed in the customs area. Oh, wait, may they successfully apply for visas and passports and get cheap flights...

I set up a kind of running tab with God as I don't remember ever saying "Amen" until I received a call from my parents that they'd safely landed back in California after a week-long adventure. But I'm getting a little ahead of myself.

After unanswered pleas to visit me during my first year in China, my parents decided to visit in May, 2008. This is a great month to visit Xinzheng, because it wasn't too cold, and the humidity was months away. As hard as it had been to convince them to come, I knew it would be astronomically harder for them to carry out the necessary steps to take the trip. They needed to get passports, visas, and plane tickets using a computer they didn't even know how to use just a year earlier. When I left for China, my parents purchased a personal computer. They had no clue even how to turn it on. Using colored stickers, I created an overly detailed how-to list to turn the computer on, reach email, read and write email, sign out and power off. Anything outside of that list, they were on their own.

...and help them figure out the websites...

By some miracle—and two trips to the Chinese consulate in San Francisco—my parents had passports and visas to visit the Middle Kingdom. They told me about their success via a Skype call.

"We could have gotten it done in one day but we got there too late," mom informed me.

"Yeah, but a trip into the city is nice."

"Sure," she continued, "and we got our plane tickets last night about midnight. We've never done it before and they cost so much money...we weren't sure. Dad and I went back and forth about whether we should hit 'purchase' or not. We just weren't sure."

"But you did, right?"

"Oh, yeah, and we're all set."

My parents were flying into Beijing on Friday, May 9, and staying through the next weekend. Since I had classes Monday through Wednesday, I decided to stay in the capital city that weekend and fly back to Xinzheng on Sunday night with my parents. I planned to use my parents for show and tell in my classrooms and then show them the Henan sights for several days before flying back to Beijing for one last night before sending them back home.

Using a computer was the first of many firsts for my parents. While my dad had sailed around the Pacific Ocean thanks to a stint in the U.S. Navy, with several stops in Asia, my mom had traveled as far west as Hawaii. She was heading west again, but adding seven hours to the flight time and this destination did not include a four-star resort.

Hey, Papa, it's me, Kim. Please, add "find an acceptable hotel room, non-spicy food, and cool breezes" to the list...

It's not that my mom is a clean freak. It's just that she really likes things clean. I don't remember every hotel or motel we stayed at on countless road trips throughout my childhood, but I do recall several motels that seemed fine from the outside that mom deemed shady and would not take a room without seeing it first. If the room did not pass her inspection—regardless of how late or tired we were—we continued down the road. It's safe to say she probably saved us from bedbugs and worse all those times.

...please let me find a good, clean room...

The baton was now in my hands and I would have to se-
lect lodging for all of us. My teacher's salary would easily cover
an upscale hostel, but my parents wouldn't go for that on the
name "hostel" alone. I wouldn't be able to get a room at any
five-, four- or three-star hotel. However, the lowest accommo-
dations foreigners were allowed to stay were two-star lodgings,
and that I could afford.

A quick visit to Charlie's office at the university got me a nice
hotel near the top attractions in Beijing: The Forbidden City,
the Summer Palace, and Tiananmen Square. The Great Wall
was also on my to-do list but it's not near anything. With my
family history firmly burned in my brain, I took a train to the
capital early Thursday. It was a good thing I did, because the
hotel room was not quite right.

The hotel was clean, which in China is tough, Beijing especially. The city battles high pollution and the occasional sand
storm. On many trips there, I felt like I was in a sandblasting
wind tunnel. The outside looked like every other building, the
reception area was neat and orderly, but the room was not as
promised.

I told Charlie I wanted a suite or a room with a separate area
for me, so we could have space. I'd been living on my own for a
while and my parents' snoring could wake the dead. He assured
me the room we booked would be fine. Fine is the Chinese way
of saying, "You may think you want this more expensive thing,
but you can get along fine with this less expensive version."

It was not fine. This was a standard-size room with two
queen beds.

After seeing the room, I asked in my best Mandarin if they
had a bigger room.

"You meiyou da fangjian, ma." Have not have big room?

Thankfully, one of the receptionists had solid English skills and the conversation advanced beyond the kindergarten level. She told me, yes, there was a larger room that had a king-size bed and then a living area with a couch.

"That one, yes, please."

"You cannot."

"I can pay the difference."

"You cannot change rooms."

"Why?"

"Because you did not book the room."

"But I did, that's my name," I said pointing to the receipt Charlie had given me.

"No, the room is booked through this agent," she replied pointing to Charlie's name.

"So even though it's in my name and I'm paying for it, I can't change it?"

She nodded. I dialed Charlie's number.

After five minutes of discussion on the definition of fine, Charlie relented and called the hotel. For some reason, I could not just hand the lady my cellphone. Less than a minute after she hung up, I had secured a room that indeed was fine. While I was there, I also signed us up to see a Chinese acrobatic show Friday night after my parents arrived (it's best to keep people active and not let them nap to avoid jet lag) and for an air conditioned van tour on Saturday that included The Great Wall and the Ming Tombs, which also served as a spa area for Chairman Mao.

Once I had my parents all set, I meandered down the way to a hostel where I would enjoy the night in a private room for about $10. It showed me how far I'd come in eighteen months. My first time in the city, I didn't want to go anywhere without a travel buddy, but now, I felt perfectly safe on my own.

Beijing International Airport made Los Angeles International look small, and that's not an easy task. I did my best to convince my parents to walk as much as possible and pack as little as possible for the trip. It's not easy lugging lots of baggage around, especially when taxis seemed designed for skinny people and thin bags. My family, like our luggage, has bulges.

It was not hard to spot two middle-aged, pasty Caucasians with bewildered looks in a sea of Asians. After unwrapping myself from their hugs, I hustled us to the taxi stand and we were soon hotel bound. It was the perfect welcome to China as the taxi weaved in and out of traffic nearly sideswiping every other car. Along the way, dad joyously pointed out a man leading a donkey that pulled a cart stacked high with furniture along the side of the freeway. The other fun find was the street sweeper that used straw brooms instead of the industrial, plastic bristle wheels like those in the States.

Mom didn't ask for a room change upon our arrival, so we prepared for the evening's entertainment. The dinner and talent show were well received by my parents. The performances included feats of strength, acrobats, and a troupe of youngsters who juggled hats. Despite the loud Asian-style music that for me hit some awkward high notes, I could see my parents were starting to nod off toward the end. The ride to the hotel was uneventful, and they were both asleep shortly after their heads hit the pillows.

...Thank you, Lord, for a great day...

Before they arrived in China, I warned my parents about the sights, smells, and squatty potties. They encountered some of the sights and a hint of smells, but as we headed out for our adventure to the tombs and wall, I reiterated my warning. I wanted them prepared to avoid the "Ugly American" stereotype.

"Also, remember that people will point and stare and laugh at you because you're a foreigner and you're heavy."

"That's rude."

"Not here, not really. Just don't get us into something my horrible Chinese can't get us out of."

I should have added "and it really can't get us out of much."

The tour left from our hotel lobby. Our guide spoke great English, and the van even had air conditioning. There were five other people in the ten-person van with us. The executive-style van had large windows for unobstructed views as we wove our way through the city towards our destinations.

The Ming Tombs were our first stop, and were a nice, slow start for my parents. It was also a first for me. In fact, if it hadn't been on the tour, I doubt I'd ever have visited. It was fun to walk around and see the ancient architecture and take in the stunning paint colors. The reds, blues, and greens on the various gates and door frames stood out against the blue-gray sky. There was a section in the back that used to house pools that Chairman Mao used to relax and rejuvenate.

What happened next, I'd totally forgotten was part of Chinese tourism. The hard sell. After getting on the van, it went just a few blocks and stopped at a special jade shop. I first encountered this see-a-sight, buy-a-trinket tour style in Xi'An, where the tour talked about the tradition of terracotta tiles and then took us to a tilemaker. I nearly smacked myself on the head when we stopped and the tour guide said, "You can now get your own jade just like the emperor's." I was glad we did not stay long, and mom was not a big fan of jade or being railroaded, so we didn't spend any money. (That would happen later at the Silk Market.)

Once we were underway again, my excitement started to grow. This would be my third trip to The Great Wall. I'd been twice to the Mutianyu section—when I first arrived in 2006, and when my cousin Pat visited in 2007. Aside from the amazing toboggan slide at Mutianyu, the thing I remember most is the long and arduous climb just to reach the gondola to take us to the wall. I knew that wouldn't work for my parents. I wanted this to be a great experience. I needed them to have fun, to enjoy themselves, to not regret having spent all that money to come halfway around the world.

There are several places tourists can access The Great Wall. Some are very remote and still covered with vegetation, but there is also a place that has super easy access: Badaling. This is where our van was headed. Unlike the other sights, Badaling's parking lot was the same height as the bottom step of the wall, literally, a person steps off the asphalt and on to thousand-year-old steps. The bad side of Badaling's easy-on, easy-off access is that it attracts scores of visitors. My parents and I added our trio to the ever-growing throng.

I stopped my parents at the bottom step, ran up several steps and then did the ultimate touristy thing: I took a picture as they took their first steps on The Wall. They were both all smiles. It didn't take too many steps on the steep and uneven stairs to change their facial expressions. I stopped and waited for them on the first landing. Mom looked like she was done, but dad appeared to have a little gas left in the tank.

"You okay, Mom?"

"Those women are pointing and laughing at me. I know what you're thinking," she said as she pointed to a group of older Chinese women. "They're laughing and saying, 'I'm fat.'"

"Probably, but I told you that would happen. Don't worry about them."

"It's rude."

"Yeah, told you that's not so much here. It's okay. Let's go a little more."

But there was no cajoling her further up the hillside, she was happy to have taken the steps she had and would wait for dad and me in the shade. Dad and I started off again, but it wasn't too long that I could tell he was done, too. In both of their defenses, they were less than twenty-four hours from finishing a thirteen-hour flight. Dad and I headed back down and found mom on the "ground floor."

The nice thing about this area is there are so many sights to see without climbing a lot. We inspected various armories, lookout posts, and took in stunning views of deep green hills. The Wall sat atop the hills and climbed and descended along the ridges for as far as our eyes could see.

Our allotted time was coming to a close, so we headed back to the van with time to spare. I wasn't going to chance being left that far from our hotel. The ride back took a different route, so we saw more of the city. After a full day of adventure, we retired for the night. I relaxed in bed thinking about getting a taxi to the airport, about the flight to my little village of Xinzheng, and about finding Julian, who said he'd meet us and take us to the university.

…let the flight be on time and cover our trip with peace and safety…

Although my parent's visit was going even better than I could have hoped, I was nervous as we boarded the plane south. For the past eighteen months, I'd lived in a community that my parents had only heard of from my emails and phone calls. On the flipside, my community knew only what I told them about my family. These worlds were about to collide, and I was a bit nervous.

I knew my parents were still a bit apprehensive about my "church life." In Sacramento, we'd attended the same mega-church since the early 1990s. I enjoyed my time there, but I had grown to love my micro-community that knew me, prayed with me, sang with me, cried with me, laughed with me. I wasn't sure how all the parties involved would mesh.

...may the spirit of community flow freely and hearts be open to new experiences...

...and, also, Papa, please, as little turbulence as possible in the air—and on the ground works, too...

The one thing I was certain was the week in Henan with my parents would be one packed with as many great memories as I could whip up for us. I convinced my parents to come to the second part of all my classes, which was as much for my students to practice their English as it was for me not to have to lesson plan for two nearly hourlong sessions. In addition, I'd coordinated with Julian, the unofficial leader of the Six Pack, to have dinner with the group at the Sias Café, sort of a high-end Outback or a low-end Ruth's Chris steak house. Julian also helped me secure a car and driver to visit the world-renowned Shaolin Temple in nearby Dengfeng.

Julian arranged for a car to pick us up at the Zhengzhou International Airport. He was waiting for us in the terminal as we came out of the baggage claim area. While his written and spoken English were impeccable, Julian was still a Chinese young man, who was not accustomed to hugging strangers. My mom, who felt like she knew him from all the stories I had shared, is a big hugger.

"Hi, Julian, thanks for picking us up."

"Not a problem."

As I introduced my parents to Julian, my mother wrapped him in a giant bear hug. His arms were pinned to his sides and he face wore the same expression it did when I'd spring a quiz on the class. He shook it all off as a crazy American custom and gathered up their bags. I carried my own pack.

When we arrived at the university, he helped my parents get settled into their guest room. They would be staying in one of the dorm rooms in the international student building. Their room was set up similar to mine: it featured a living area with couches and chairs as you entered the room. The bathroom—with required Western-style toilet was just off the small hallway, which also had low cabinets with a microwave and mini-fridge. The bedroom was in the back. It had a spacious closet and little balcony area with a small table and chairs, and the balcony overlooked the main entry square for the college. There was a fountain in the middle of the square that acted as a roundabout. My first class of the week was the building just on the other side of the square.

Once they unpacked and washed, we headed for my room in the foreign teacher's building. We were in time for dinner and Sunday night worship service. The meeting was held in the conference room just off the dining hall. With the guitars and drums, it sounded like the church they were used to in California. The prayers and message were also on point. As friends met my parents and talked with us afterward, I could see the acceptance on my parent's faces. They knew I was in a safe place, surrounded by the unconditional love of community and God.

...thank you for a safe flight and great day. Please, continue to cover us with your hand of grace...

Being the great daughter that I am, I planned to let my parents sleep in the next morning. However, when I came down to the dining hall for breakfast, there was dad already enjoying a meal and coffee. I walked him back to his room and went over how to use the laundry facilities with mom. We took a quick run through the local market on campus to get them the essentials: Oreos, Coke, and Kraft crackers.

My first class of the day came after lunch, which in China meant two o'clock. It seemed the entire country took a two-hour nap after the noon meal. The first class after lunch was rough, because typically, half the students were still groggy and stumbled through the door. Add to that, the class was "American Culture Through Film"—meaning it was dark every other week watching movies—and some kids caught four-hour naps.

The back building was one of the first built on the decade-old campus, and it was already crumbling in parts. The dais area had broken tiles that had me tiptoeing around, and several pull-down blinds were askew. The room heated quickly from the morning sun and by the afternoon it was sweltering, but there was no air conditioning. The windows were left ajar to help air circulate, which allowed the sounds of dump trucks going back and forth to the garbage heap to roll in with the smells. It was not my favorite room.

That afternoon, I reminded my students that we'd have normal discussion the first fifty minutes and then I'd go get my parents at the break and bring them in for a second-half Q&A. They broke out in massive applause, which I interpreted as being happy to meet my parents and overjoyed to not have to listen to a lecture.

I cannot remember what movie we were discussing, whether we were looking at genre, plot or characters, but I vividly recall the first sign something was wrong.

"Teacher!"

I turned to see a female student standing. It was rare for a student to speak without raising a hand. It was nearly unheard of for them to stand and shout.

"Excuse me."

"Teacher, we are having an earthquake!"

"No, we are not. Please, sit down."

I was arrogantly thinking, *Dude, I'm a native Californian. I've lived through numerous earthquakes. Tell me we're having an earthquake.*

"It is true! See? It is moving," she said pointing to the projection screen. The other students were starting to get agitated. I wasn't sure if it was because they agreed with her or were nervous by her actions.

"It was just a big truck coming by. That's all."

"No. It was an earthquake."

I paused to think. What if she was right? What were the safety procedures in place to follow? Then a cold feeling swept over me as I realized the university had never ever given us a fire drill evacuation plan. There wasn't a plan in place. My inner middle-school safety monitor kicked in...

"Okay, if there was an earthquake," I said, still unbelieving, "we need to leave together and stay together until the administration gives the all clear to re-enter the building. Please, in an orderly fashion gather your belongings, and line up at the door."

Yes, it was weird asking college sophomores to line up at the door, but it was what my earliest training taught me.

"We will go down the stairs on the right and continue to the fountain. It's important that we stay together as a class."

I was fully expecting us to walk out into an empty hallway and courtyard area. My students may have thought I'd lost my mind but I was still the teacher and in China that carries a lot of respect. They grabbed their things and got in two lines.

As I opened the door, I was overwhelmed by the sea of people rushing by me, some shouting, all running. I turned to see my organized students catching a glimpse of the same scene and watched their eyes glaze in panic.

They all started to run, some down the right stairs, others to the left.

"Hey, come back! We have to stay together," I yelled to no one listening. I did manage to snag the arm of my class monitor and keep him with me. "We're going to the fountain."

My parents were resting in the living area of their room. Suddenly, there was a shift in the room. The water sloshed in the gallon jug on the dispenser. A crack appeared in the ceiling and snaked its way across the room.

In talking to them afterward, my parents knew two things: One, that there had been a major earthquake somewhere, and two, that I was probably going to be slow to react. They didn't place any wagers, but made their way to the back balcony overlooking the fountain square and waited to see how long it would be until I came out.

In my defense, I grew up in Southern California. When I was four years old, a 6.5 magnitude earthquake rocked the San Gabriel Mountains and violently shook our two-story home. It was like walking through a carnival fun house where the floor shifted out from under you. It was kind of a fun sensation for me, even though the adults were quite frantic.

We moved to the Bay Area in my mid-teens and felt even more quakes. In high school, I literally saw the earth move in tiny waves as I was putting the bases on the softball field for a game later that day. I was kneeling to hammer the metal stake when I suddenly felt nauseous and lifted my head to see the ground going up and down in three-inch ripples. I fell back on to my butt.

"Dude, I think I'm going to be sick," I yelled at my friend Janet, who was mowing the grass and was not fazed by anything.

"Huh?" She turned off the motor.

That's when we heard the shouting and looked toward our high school building to see students and teachers streaming out on to the field area.

"Earthquake," we said in unison.

Easily my favorite seismic encounter was not long after, but this time it was at night. As an only child, I'll admit, I was a bit spoiled. Otherwise, why else would I have a queen-size water-bed. One night, I was jostled awake by my bed as it undulated wildly. Since I didn't see anyone pushing on it, I figured it was an earthquake, and since I was enjoying the sensation, I didn't see a reason to get out of bed.

"Kim! Are you okay?" came mom's voice from down the hall.

"Yes."

"Are you out of bed and in a safe place?"

"No."

"Kimberly Ann!"

"Alright."

Reluctantly, I got out of bed and sat at the bottom of the door frame. Ironically, decades later, people in the know said that wasn't a safe place to be. I would have been just as safe if I had stayed put.

Once I reached the fountain area, I determined about half my class was there. There were dozens of other students in the area. Everyone was on their cell phone, checking in with family. I turned to wave at my parents.

"We need to get all the others here," I said to the class monitor.

"I do not know where they are."

"I know. We can look around the other side of the building, but you also need to text them. I need to see that they are safe."

He shook his head and started punching the phone keys. It took about another fifteen minutes to get the class together by the fountain. I took roll and marked everyone safe as my inner safety monitor glowed with delight.

The students began sharing videos and news posts. The devastation in the Sichuan area was beyond measure. The southwest province was hammered by an 8.0 earthquake. The loss of life was staggering. More than 68,000 people died in the initial hit, and that number grew as rescue crews scoured for more than 18,000 missing souls. The epicenter was more than 800 miles from our province, but students heard from family members all over China who felt the initial quake and were rocked by the aftershocks.

Students and staff members milled about waiting for someone to tell us what to do next. The impact of the tragedy put us into a stupor. Eventually, an administrator came over and let us know classes were canceled for the day.

I made my way to my parent's room where we talked about the day's events and recalled the earthquakes we'd been through together. *Together* was the key word. Not that my parents were over protective, but they were over protective and excessive worriers. Although I wasn't happy that they had experienced another earthquake, I was relieved that they were with me. I shuddered to think of the worry they would be going through if they were in California hearing of such a tragic event. They wouldn't have cared—or known—that the epicenter was thirteen hours away by car. All they would see, like us, were pictures of toppled buildings, inconsolable people and overtaxed rescue squads.

...Be with the people of Sichuan. Thank you for keeping all of us safe. Thank you for helping me find all my students. Grant us peace...

Classes were back on track by the next day. My parents sat awkwardly at the front of the class like show monkeys and answered question after question.

I was not surprised by the questions: How old are you? How long have you been married? What do you do in America? However, I was a bit taken aback by who was asking them. Students whom I wasn't even sure understood English raised their hands and engaged in conversation. It hurt my feelings a bit that they decided my parents were worthy of their orations and not me, but as with all the other small things that felt like slights, I brushed it off and just enjoyed the joy in the moment.

There were times my parents and I clashed, but honestly, they were some of the coolest people I knew. Their sense of adventure was not as keen as mine, but the spirit of hospitality and generosity abounded with them. They were always opening our home to me and whatever ragtag group of friends I was with at the time.

When we were planning their trip, I came up with the sightseeing sections, and my folks were all about get-togethers. Along with meeting my community of friends, they were most excited to meet the infamous Six Pack. I'd been sharing pictures and stories of Julian, Michael, Kevin, Jack, Shellie, and Sue since my first semester. The sextet made me their personal cultural exchange project.

They taught me to make *jiaozi* (dumplings) that first winter before I returned home for Christmas. Michael, who said he was putting a peanut in the stuffing and the person who found it would have good luck, found the peanut. We were all sure he cheated and marked the dumpling.

They taught me how to play *mahjong*. We played for cookies and not for money.

They took me on bike rides around the city and showed me all the local cultural landmarks. They worked on improving my Chinese. Mostly, they just made life more enjoyable for me. They were students turned friends. My parents could hardly wait to meet them all. They met Julian at the airport, much to the chagrin of the other five.

There were numerous restaurants off campus that served amazing dishes that we had dined at before my parent's visit. However, my parents wanted to do something special, and so we set a time to meet at the Sias Café on campus. This East-meets-West restaurant was easily the fanciest outside of the metropolis of Zhengzhou. It was also the priciest. One drink at the café was more than an entire meal at some places. My parents, who were firmly middle-class, never had loads of money or flaunted what they did have, but they loved to shower gifts on people when they could, and with the U.S. dollar going at about seven-to-one against the Chinese RMB, they certainly made it rain.

We arranged for a time to meet at the restaurant. The first clue that it was going to be a great night was that we all arrived at the same time. I introduced my parents to my friends, and by everyone's beaming expressions, it was hard to tell who was more excited to meet whom.

"Kim, I must tell you something," said Michael, the jokester of the group. "I have not eaten anything all day, *and* I went swimming to make sure I was very hungry and had room to put it."

He wasn't kidding. It seemed as if all of them had taken similar courses of action. They were thumbing through a menu that would give The Cheesecake Factory a run for its money on heftiness.

"Order whatever you want," my parents told them over and over. "Don't worry about anything."

"May we get drinks?" the girls asked in near unison, giggling behind their hands.

"Whatever you want."

This was a big deal because typically when we'd gone out, drinks consisted of the free tea provided by the restaurant. It was rare for them to get a soft drink or milk tea. It was also rare for them to be having an American-style meal, so they were a bit overwhelmed.

When the waiter came to take the order, my parents and I were pretty straightforward. Things took a comical turn when he got to the Six Pack. First, they all started talking in Mandarin and then admonishing each other to use English. By the time all the ordering was done for nine people, we had twelve entrees, nine desserts, six milk teas, fives sides, and three soft drinks. The waiter looked at my parents who gave him a thumbs up—it's a very handy gesture.

In between bites of food, they shared about their days in the classroom, tattled on me for various offenses in the classroom, and asked my parents all the questions they'd been asked by all my classes. My parents answered them all again like champs.

As the plates were being cleared, my mom wanted to give each of them a gift. They were confused because they thought dinner was their gift. She had asked me before leaving Sacramento what should she get them.

"They don't need anything. The dinner will be more than fine for them."

"Kimberly Ann, they need gifts."

We went round and round about what was an appropriate gift. We settled on her final item because it was also practical.

"It's just a little something for all of you," said Mom as she pulled a small box from her purse. "We got them in San Francisco for you."

She handed the package to Julian, who removed the lid to reveal six ballpoint pens with a variety of iconic San Francisco tourist spots on them. You'd have thought she'd given them all bars of gold. It was a very happy table. They brought dad the bill, and when he saw it I quickly let him know what it was in U.S. dollars, and he laughed.

"What's so funny?" mom asked.

"All this," he said moving his hand to take in the table, "all this food was like a hundred bucks."

"What?"

"Right," I piped up. "It's made it hard for me to eat out in California because I keep thinking, 'Dang, I could have had five meals for this in Zhengzhou.'"

The Six Pack was oblivious to our discussion, as they were busy comparing pens and already using them to write on any piece of paper they could find.

The only person who seemed ready for the night to end was me, because I've known my parents my whole life and I see the Six Pack every week. It took several attempts to say goodbye outside the café, but finally, they headed off toward their dorms and I corralled my parents toward theirs.

"Oh, I'm going to miss them."

"Julian is going with us to the Shaolin Temple tomorrow."

"Oh, that's wonderful."

"Plan A" had been for Julian to help me arrange transportation and tickets for my parents and I to the Shaolin Temple in nearby Dengfeng. I figured I could manage for our travel with my broken Mandarin. Turns out Julian figured differently, so he came up with "Plan B."

He arranged for a car and tickets for all of us to take the one-hour drive together. Julian secured the top choice for foreigners when they traveled: Superman. While he didn't wear a cape or glasses, the owner of the convenience store had grown into the title over the years for his amazing service and ability to procure what expats needed. My first year, he had an average size car. Now, just over a eighteen months later, he had a massive luxury car that doubled as a taxi. I felt I'd helped the overall gross national product of Xinzheng.

Julian and Superman greeted us outside the teacher's apartment building. I noticed Julian ran around to the side of the car to open the door for my mom. I thought that was sweet of him as I opened my own door. On the way there, Julian gave a brief history of the Shaolin monks, the development of their specialized Kung Fu, and movies starring Jackie Chan and Jet Li. The terrain changed a lot about midway there as the road started to climb into the tree-lined hills. I enjoyed leaving behind the flat farmland of Xinzheng.

My first visit to the temple area was a university field trip that gave us access to the lower grounds and one of the Kung Fu demonstrations. "Plan A" had been to get my parents the same package, but, again, Julian had a "Plan B." He wanted to get a special package that not only would allow us to see what I had before, but added on a chairlift ride up the mountains for more trails and better views. I was eager to see something new, too, so he received no arguments from me.

The Shaolin Temple grounds were vast and covered with red-roofed buildings, tall pine trees, and a pagoda cemetery. The buildings housed the monks and students, most of whom would end up working in the entertainment field and not become spiritual leaders. There were numerous Shaolin troupes that traveled the country and the world performing martial arts.

Long before the movie *Kung Fu Panda*, the Shaolin masters demonstrated moves dubbed "the crane," "the snake," "the tiger," and "the frog," to name a few. Many of the martial arts moves were derived from observing nature. There were also demonstrations with knives, spears, and nunchucks. From all the "ooohs" and "aaaws," it was obvious my parents loved the show.

On our way to the chairlift, we meandered through the cemetery that featured pagodas instead of traditional western headstones. The more important the monk, the taller his pagoda. There were many important teachers, and the pagodas formed their own forest within the trees.

It was a warm day, and the gentle breeze through the trees as we took the chairlift was refreshing. Julian and I were ahead of my parents. I could hear them talking but couldn't make out what they were saying, but when I turned around, all I could see were smiles, so it must have been a good conversation.

We reached what I thought was the top of the mountain, but Julian informed me that there was more hiking to do. I knew my parents weren't going to walk too far, but since these were sloped trails and not the awkward stairs of The Great Wall, I figured they'd be okay for a little while. For about the first mile, we all walked together. However, when Julian spotted the turn-off for the mountain summit and explained the remaining hike, my parents opted to sit on the nearby bench and enjoy the view as we continued upward.

As the path continued up, it eventually broke through the tree line to massive rock outcroppings. The end of the trail was marked by a giant sign that resembled a tombstone. If it had been any farther, I may have died. Julian and I took our obligatory photos with the sign, and took in the view of the valley far below. If it was a clear day, we might have seen Xinzheng. (I knew from home on a clear day, we could see the mountains we were standing among.)

We met up with my parents and headed back down. I noticed Julian hanging back and walking and chatting with my mom. When we arrived at the chairlift, he joined me for the trip down. Again we were in front and stepped off first at the bottom of the hill. Julian quickly moved back to my parent's chair as it entered the disembark station and reached out to help my mom off the chair. The kid was making me look bad.

Superman took the express turnpike on the way home. The blacktop of the recently finished six-lane highway was pristine. My parents, who had lived in the Los Angeles area for more than a decade, were shocked. They had never seen such an empty or pot-hole free stretch of highway.

We arrived home well ahead of our scheduled time. After the appropriate "thanks" and "goodbyes" with Superman, we took Julian out for pizza and said our goodbyes since we'd be leaving early the next day. Of course that was "Plan A." Julian's "Plan B" had him there waiting with the taxi when we came down the next morning. Everyone said their goodbyes again, and mom got into the taxi. The next thing I knew, Julian crawled in there and gave her a giant hug. That's when I knew I had a Chinese younger brother. (Little did we know, in five years, he'd be visiting us in California for Christmas, and it would be my turn to play tour guide.)

It was time to play tourist again as we returned to Beijing for my parents final twenty-four hours in China. There were a few things they needed to see before boarding the big bird to the U.S.: Tiananmen Square, The Forbidden City, and the Silk Market.

Walking around the giant square surrounded by imposing government buildings, it's very easy to feel small—which I think is the point of it all. I pointed out various points of interest and recalled the historical significance of the square. I reminded them of the 1989 massacre where political demonstrators and bystanders were overrun by military forces. It's also been the sight of numerous protests that never made any news program or paper. It has the same draw as the Capitol Mall in Washington D.C.; it's where people go to be seen by their government and air their grievances. There is a somberness to the place that is weighed down even more by the massive buildings.

We moved slowly through the crowds of people. Even on a cool day, the square heats quickly with body heat, ground heat, and reflected heat from the buildings. I led us toward the Forbidden City and didn't see a tall Chinese man come up and start talking to my dad. I assumed we were all together and kept talking to no one but myself at the time. I turned to ask a question.

"What do you think?" I asked, turning. I was a bit stunned to realize my parents were not beside me. I scanned the area and saw them about thirty feet away. I hurried back to them as the man was leaving.

"Everything okay?" I asked. "What happened?"

"He wanted to give us a tour," Dad said. "I told him, 'No thank you, we have a tour guide.'"

"You got a tour guide?"

"Yes. You," he said.

I was grateful for the compliment and the faith my parents had in me to get them from Point A to Point B.

It was my third visit to The Forbidden City, former home of the emperor. In a way, it's the Chinese version of Mt. Vernon. The emperor slept here; George Washington ate there. It was nice to be leading a tour so I kept myself engaged by passing on all the little tidbits I'd learned or things I did on previous visits.

I regaled them with the time I visited with Pat the previous year. My cousin Pat was three years younger than me. Our first big outing as cousins happened when I was eight and he was five. My dad took us to see the movie *Jaws*. We were both scared but loved it. That same trip, we caught a Dodgers game with the Boys in Blue winning, so he joined me in my fandom. We continued to take trips together as we grew older. I visited him in Virginia; both of us traveled to Florida to see another cousin; and we took in a week of spring training games in central Florida. So it did not surprise me when he said he'd like to visit me in China.

Pat came at the end of my first year of teaching. We met in Shanghai first, took in the Bund area and visited Suzhou;

then it was a fast train ride to Beijing for more adventure. The one thing he'd mentioned several times was wanting to find the Starbucks in The Forbidden City. I thought it was a myth, but he was certain it existed. He was eager to drink a toast to capitalism creeping its way into the heart of communism. There was something a bit rebellious about the idea, and even though I'm not a big fan of coffee, I do enjoy the occasional scandal.

We looked in nearly every nook and cranny of nearly all the 999 rooms of The Forbidden City and were just about to give up when we saw a couple of women carrying plastic cups with the unmistakable green logo. We rushed over to them and asked for directions.

"Back over the bridge, but if you reach the next bridge you've gone too far..."

I was having flashbacks of trying to follow Katie's directions for my first bike ride. I shook the memory from my mind to focus.

"...You'll see the sign for the toilets, go that way, but before you get there you'll see a bookstore. It's in there."

"The bathroom is in the bookstore?"

"No, no," she said with a nervous laugh. "The Starbucks is in the bookstore."

Armed with these amazing and vague directions, we set off to find the elusive caffeine provider. After backtracking when we hit the second bridge, we paid more attention as we retraced our steps. We both saw the sign for books at about the same time, slapping each other's shoulders.

"There's the bookstore," we chimed.

"But I don't see a Starbucks' sign," I said with a sigh.

"Maybe they know inside," Pat said as he headed for the building. Once he opened the door, we knew we were in the right place. The aroma of roasted beans was overwhelming, and the line of people that snaked through the bookstore aisles let us know we were not the only people seeking this experience. There was minimal signage inside the building as well. The green aprons and logoed cups the only signs. We ordered our various concoctions; I opted for a cooler smoothie on the warm June day.

About three months later, Pat emailed me a link to a story saying the location had finally been shut down. Granted, people can get Starbucks nearly everywhere in China still, but there is something memorable in knowing that Pat and I were among the few who tracked down the forbidden drink.

There would be no such hunting with my parents. I set a nice leisurely pace that allowed us to see the most of the expansive monument area. There were several stores that sold miniature versions of the city, T-shirts emblazoned with Mao or a giant red star, and multicolored umbrellas and scrolls. I convinced my parents to save their money for the Silk Market, which has a larger variety and is a better place to bargain.

Bargaining is a sport in China. It is a sport I don't always enjoy playing. If I'm in the mood and feeling feisty, I'll battle a merchant to save money. My students were always in the mood to bargain and would be upset with me if I didn't push hard enough.

"That is not worth more than five yuan."

"I paid six."

They would shake their heads and look at me as if I were crazy. One yuan or renminbi (RMB) was worth about twelve U.S. cents at the time. In my mind, it wasn't worth it. In my student's minds, it was half the cost of lunch. Perspective is important in China.

The perspective of merchants in the Silk Market was that all foreigners had just stepped off jumbo jets with hundreds of dollars in their pockets, ripe for the picking. As someone living in China and being paid in RMB, it's important to establish your situation early.

"*Wo shi laoshi. Wo zhu zai zheli. Xiang xia yige waiguoren shouqu geng duo feiyong.*" (I'm a teacher. I live here. Charge the next foreigner more.) And it usually helped knock the price considerably. And I didn't feel badly for any of the Americans paying full price because they still thought they were getting a great deal.

On Pat's visit, my friends Jen and Barbie were with us. Barbie was a recent graduate from Sias and had amazing English skills. While we were in the market, Pat saw a stunning chopstick set that was listed at one thousand yuan. Pat was trying his best to negotiate—sellers use a calculator display to tell you the price if you don't understand Chinese. Pat and the seller were pushing that calculator back and forth. Finally, Barbie stepped in and started negotiating on Pat's behalf. She whittled the price down to forty RMB. A savings of 960 yuan! As we walked away, the only Mandarin I could make out was he called Barbie "a bad Chinese person." She wasn't fazed by it. "I bargained well."

There was no Barbie with me this time. I would sink or overpay all on my own. The first thing to know about the Silk Market is that it's more than silk. It is a giant big-box store broken down into cubicles of various wares, including handbags, scarves, toys, games, luggage, jewelry, and many other trinkets and souvenirs. I asked mom what she wanted to see and we found ourselves in the pearl market section. All the sellers have pretty much the same inventory and sales tactics. They scrape the pearls; try to set them on fire; it's quite a show. Before we picked out what she wanted, I asked her how much she was willing to pay.

"One hundred," she informed me.

"Sounds good to me." And it did. It's a number I knew how to pronounce, and it's a nice price point. In hindsight, it's possible my mom was thinking $100, which would have been about 700 RMB. But I took it as one hundred RMB and a solid challenge for my bargaining skills.

We found a three-piece set that she liked and let the games begin. The hard part of having 100 as an end point was tossing out really low numbers like forty or fifty for a starting point.

"You are taking food from my children," the seller said, pushing the calculator toward me with 900 even though I'd used pretty good Chinese to indicate my opening bid.

"You will find a way. You are a good father. *Wushi-wu*," I said pushing back the device with fifty-five on it.

"You insult me. These are fine pearls," he said as once again he set to scraping and burning them. "See?" He was down to 800.

This went back and forth until I hit *yibai*, 100. He would not come down, and I could not go up.

"*Wode mama shuo yibai*," I said pointing at my mom, who had been instructed to nod and give "the look."

He looked at my mom, at me, and then came down to 300. I didn't even let him pass the calculator all the way back.

"*Wode mama...*" and then he realized "my mama" wasn't going to budge and we left with the spoils of our bargain battle.

As we ate dinner that night, I asked my parents what they had liked or been surprised by the most.

"You made it sound like it would be really rough, but I haven't even had to use a squatty potty once," my mom said.

...*Dear God, you really came through...*

Maybe too good.

I'd been praying so hard and so long for my parents to have the greatest trip ever, and now that it had happened and they were getting ready to go home happy, I was annoyed. They hadn't experienced any of the inconveniences that I'd lived with for the past eighteen months. And as much as that's what I'd prayed for and that's what I wanted, what I really wanted then was to make them suffer just a little bit.

...*Papa, forgive me for I know exactly what I am doing*...

It was a beautiful night, and I convinced them to take a final walk around and see the local night market. These are the markets seen on television filled with beetles, scorpions, and squid on a stick. There is also a delicacy in China lovingly called stinky tofu, which doesn't even begin to describe the stench. At first, there is a slight tingle in the back of the throat and a burning in the nasal cavity. The smell has a palpable weight that triggers the gag reflex and the fight-or-flight response—always go with flight.

It honestly was a wonderful night, and I almost felt bad for what I was about to do...but not that bad. We were engaged in polite conversation when I caught the first hints we were headed in the right—but, oh, so wrong—direction. My parents were about a half-step behind me as we continued down the aisle. I had to fight the flight response and press forward. It was only a second later that I heard my parents gasping for air.

"Oh, my gosh! What is that?"

"Kim, we have got to turn around."

A Cheshire grin spread across my face. "Okay, if you want to go back," I said as I whipped a U-turn, grabbed each of them by an elbow and led us away from the horrid odor. I felt better knowing we now had a true China smell to unite us.

Their final hours in China went smoothly as I took them to the airport and walked them as far as I could. We said our goodbyes with lots of hugs and tears. It had been a wonderful trip, and I was a bit sad to see them leave.

...Thank you, God, for such a great time. Please, extend travel mercies and may they have good dinner options...

I was back on my own as I left the terminal, but some of my friends were in town, so I joined them and continued my China adventure.

It wasn't until the next day that I heard from my parents. In addition to the fifteen-hour time difference, their connecting flight from San Francisco to Sacramento was overbooked. The airline offered money and my parents took it and a later flight, a much later flight. They ended up waiting nearly eight hours— enough time to have driven back and forth twice between the cities.

It was good to hear their voices and know they were finally home safe and sound.

Thank you so very much, Papa, for such a memorable experience and for getting my folks home safe. Amen

CHAPTER 20

RAISING THE DEAD: STUDENT HOME VISIT, PART II

While it seemed every student wanted to be my friend during the semesters I taught them, Annabelle and Eileen were serious about maintaining a relationship even after I stopped being their teacher.

As translation majors, the duo had amazing English skills that extended to a strong grasp of idioms and slang. I was spoiled by their hard work. We could have conversations about everything in a nice easy pace, while my friends who taught physical education or Chinese literature majors, struggled to communicate without clear and drawn-out pronunciation.

Annabelle and Eileen were nearly inseparable. They took all but one class together, and I rarely saw one without the other. Annabelle sparkled with her high energy storytelling and eclectic clothing style. Eileen was cerebral, calculated, and quick with a joke but conservative in dress and verbiage. I came to attribute it to how many words Annabelle used at any given time.

Spending time with them—or any other student-turned-friend—when I was no longer their teacher was so much easier for me. I no longer had that nagging thought in the back of my head wondering if a student was just trying to find a way to a better grade.

We went out to dinner, on shopping trips (Annabelle loved to shop, while Eileen and I were there for the show) and walked through the local parks. We did so much together that it seemed poetic that my last year teaching in China was their final year at Sias. It felt like a good note to go out on for me.

Before the students left on winter break, Annabelle asked me if I'd visit her home for Spring Festival. I'd come a long way since my first year in Xinzheng, and the thought of being the only foreigner in a city no longer frightened me. (It should have.) Plus, she said her uncle had given permission for us to bring the ancestors home for the new year. I'd heard a great deal about ancestor worship in China and read of some of the customs, so it was too good an opportunity to miss.

I also must confess that based solely on her attitude and up-to-date style, I assumed Annabelle came from a big city and my holiday living conditions would be close to Linda's home life. (Yeah, made an ass out of me.)

Annabelle came to my apartment to pick me up and ride the bus with me. I told her I was an adult and could ride a bus by myself and listen for the bus stop. She laughed and grabbed my backpack. That should have been a clue.

As per usual for Spring Festival, the bus was jam-packed. There were three people in each two-person seat and a line of people in the aisle. I felt claustrophobic when a policeman climbed on to the bus and started shouting and pointing.

"He says, there are too many people on the bus," Annabelle translated for me. "Those in the center must get off."

"Those in the center" did not take the news well and yelled back. Finally, they got off the bus, and I was able to get a bit of air. The bus rolled out of the terminal and around the corner. It went maybe half a block and stopped. The bus driver opened the door and "those in the center" filed back onto the bus. Along the way, Annabelle talked about the cities we went through. She also explained that while her mom was home, her dad was still in southern China.

"He is waiting for the paychecks," she said. "The factory owner is waiting until the last minute to pay them to keep them working. My mom left early to help grandma prepare the food. Dad will get their checks and hopes to be here for Spring Festival."

As with many families, the eldest lived in the family home while others traveled for work or school and returned once a year for Spring Festival. For Annabelle, it was a short bus ride, but for her parents, the train trip could last twenty-four hours. And now that annual visit was in danger of being shorter if her dad's company didn't pay up.

As we continued on, I noticed we were in the middle of nowhere. I couldn't remember the last time I'd seen a building, which was extremely odd. China is a pragmatic, preemptive country. If the government assumes people will eventually move into a certain area, the infrastructure is all put into place—even if that means buildings go empty for years. To go several miles without seeing a real or ghost town had my Spidey senses tingling.

"We're here," she said, grabbing my bag and sidestepping the person in the aisle.

"Where?" I couldn't see anything but flat, barren land out my window. However, once I was up and moving down the aisle, on the other side I could see a few small buildings. One was a market—I knew this from the advertising in the window, not an ability to read characters—the other a phone store and the third looked like a pawn shop.

"We'll walk down the road until Uncle finds us," said Annabelle, unwilling to relinquish my bag. My face must have asked a question my voice could not since she continued, "It won't be long. Our village is thirty minutes."

She smiled and her high, round cheekbones started to turn pink from the sun and the cold.

All I could think was I'm already in the middle of nowhere, what is a half hour from here going to look like. This was the total opposite of visiting Linda in the big city, and I was suddenly starting to get nervous.

It wasn't long until Uncle found us and we piled into the little van. Annabelle eagerly chatted in Mandarin. Her face becoming more animated with each word. She occasionally paused and let Uncle speak, and then she'd translate for me. I noticed a small outcropping of homes and farms ahead. We slowed to turn into the Feng Zhuang village in Bo'Ai county.

"It is a small and peaceful village," Annabelle informed me. It reminded me of the small community near the university where I took my first bike ride.

The same families had lived and farmed and died in Feng Zhuang for generations, and approximately seventy-five percent of them bore the family name Feng. (It's like living in Smithville and the vast majority of the residents are named Smith.) There were no strangers in this village. The farmland around the walled homes was divided into sections. However, since some areas were more fertile than others, families would switch to the next plot over after a decade or so, allowing everyone an equal chance to farm good and bad land. Making things just a tad trickier with land sharing was the lack of cemeteries. The government expected individuals to be cremated, but in most rural areas, loved ones were buried on the land. I learned the next day that these burial areas, like the crops, were rotated.

We drove down the packed dirt streets and were soon outside the large gate for the family home. The overall layout was similar to Linda's, with a courtyard that was home to storage and the squatty potty. (Having to cover all that ground in the freezing night air really made me ponder how bad I really needed to use the facilities.)

Annabelle's brother gave up his room for me to stay in for the holiday. The bedroom walls were lined with posters of Asian pop stars and NBA All-Stars. The one adjustment to the room was that the family purchased a bed warmer for my visit. (It's almost as if they knew foreigners were highly susceptible to the cold.) I was honored, humbled, and, honestly, delighted to not only have a bed to myself but also an adult-size heating pad.

Grandma said something in Mandarin, all the while shaking her head and pointing at the bed and then to me.

"You must turn it off when you get into bed," Annabelle said. "She said you could catch on fire."

"Well, that would be bad."

I was a bit sad to know that I wouldn't have the heat all night, but it certainly warmed up a large section and made it easier to drift off to sleep. It felt colder the next morning as I crawled out from under the many layers of quilts. I layered nearly all the clothes I'd brought plus a down jacket and was still cold. Thankfully, there were things to do that created movement and body heat.

We spent the day helping Brother put up the new year couplet banners by staying out of his way. The signs were hand-painted by specialists with a bamboo brush. Annabelle's uncle on her mother's side was skilled with a brush, a tradition that dated back thousands of years in China. A month prior to Spring Festival, he would begin painting couplets that focused on good fortune. Some of these he would sell, others he would donate to his family members.

The long strips of red "good luck" paper featured couplets in fluid, Chinese calligraphy. They were placed on both sides of the door posts and above the mantel. The sight always reminded me of the Passover story, when the Hebrews put lamb's blood around their doors to keep firstborns from dying.

In the late afternoon, Annabelle let me know it was time to get ready to bring the ancestors home for Spring Festival. This year was particularly emotional for the family, as Grandpa passed within recent years. Grandpa's youngest brother—who was just a few years older than Uncle—returned home for New Year's Eve. He moved to the city when he was twenty to find work, but always found his way home for the yearly festival.

Annabelle felt it was a combination of the pull of tradition and Grandma's dumplings that brought him back again and again. It was obvious that Uncle was glad to see his young relative as well. The men were more like brothers than uncle and nephew.

While Mom and Grandma stayed home to finish preparing the meal, Annabelle, the uncles and I took our baskets filled with silver and gold paper and numerous rounds of fireworks to start our journey. We stopped at a store to pick up Grandpa's favorite cigarettes and liquor. Our small family group soon merged with other families carrying their own baskets. Some of the men lit firecrackers and tossed them into the air. The group grew a bit more, and the village elder took the lead. His tanned and wrinkled face was framed by a jacket with a high collar and a low-hanging knit beanie.

He motioned the group to a halt on the edge of a field where the town walls ended.

"We will now honor the first resting place of our ancestors," Annabelle translated for me. Everyone faced the field and bowed three times. Standing at the back, no one saw me remain upright. I said a little prayer for all the families, *comfort for the loss of loved ones and health for the living.*

There was a lot of bantering and more fireworks as we moved to the next burial site. The energy and excitement of the crowd was heightened with increased pyrotechnic displays. I was totally at home in cemeteries. I like to sit—yes, I've had lunch in a cemetery—and talk with friends or family members who've passed away. I find it cathartic and peaceful. No, no one talks back. But I felt as if I'd finally found a group of individuals as comfortable around the dead as I am. It was nice.

When we reached the farm area where the ancestors were buried, Annabelle and I stayed on the road, and the men went to small mounds around the area. The uncles placed the silver and gold paper on top of each mound and set it on fire.

"This sends the gold and silver to Grandpa for him to use," Annabelle explained.

"Cool," I said, noticing that not everyone burned the same amount, and wondered if the deceased would be complaining later that Grandpa got more than them.

Next, the men lit up cigarettes and placed them butt end into the ground, so it appeared someone was under the grass smoking. They opened the liquor, took a drink and then poured it around the mound, being careful not to get the cigarettes wet. The men began to weep. During my time in China, I saw men express many emotions, but sadness and grief with tears was new, and I felt as if I'd invaded some sacred moment. I was again humbled, and offered up a prayer of thanks to be included in such a personal family moment.

The quiet sobs were quickly overpowered by thousand-round firecrackers erupting around the field.

"This is to let them know it's time to wake up and go home," Annabelle said.

"It certainly woke me up," I laughed.

The peaceful farm land took on the look and feel of a war movie as the bright flashes from the fireworks shone through the ever billowing smoke clouds. The green grass was soon covered in small scraps of red paper from the firecrackers.

Then the village elder declared it was time to go home. I wasn't sure if it was because he knew everyone was awake or he, like me, was eager to start enjoying the celebratory meal. It turns out there was one more stop on the way home. We crowded into what appeared to be an abandoned home and set some fireworks off inside. There was no explanation given, and sometimes it was best to just go along for the ride.

Upon arriving at the family door, we were greeted by our amazing cooks. As a family, it was time to welcome Grandpa back for the festival. There was bowing and fireworks. We all stepped over the threshold. More bowing and fireworks. There was a final set of firecrackers outside the gate.

"To keep out the unwanted spirits," it was explained.

"Sounds like a good idea to me."

And now that we were all home, it was time to eat.

While my first home visit was great, this visit felt more intimate. Maybe it was because after five years, I felt more at home with the simplicity of Chinese life. Maybe it was because I'd known Annabelle for three years and she felt like family. Maybe it was because I truly appreciated the gift of hospitality being extended to me. Whatever the reason, sitting around the table with such an amazing spread of food and flanked by happy faces, I felt at home.

I noticed whenever Grandma brought out food for the table she stopped by Grandpa's shrine and put some food there as well. He had a bowl of oranges, some sunflower and watermelon seeds, a few apples, and some dried meats. His place of honor also contained a long blanket-like banner that featured the names of ancestors who had died. His was the newest name on the list.

Another "sacred" part of any dinner was the toast. In the States, I'd attended a few parties or weddings where champagne was used to toast various speeches. Some I liked—the champagne, that is—some I didn't, but none of them made me think, "Gee, I need more of this."

In fact, before moving to China, I could count on both hands the number of alcoholic drinks I'd had in my lifetime—champagne at weddings clicked off three digits. My grandpa tricking me into drinking beer and brandy ticked off another two. Then there were the daiquiris and mimosas I'd enjoyed at various brunches with friends.

I had to start using my toes to count not long after moving to China. While my go-to drink of choice was still any form of tea, I discovered pineapple beer (*boluo pijiu*) during my second semester of teaching. It was more fun to say than drink, but truly refreshing on an especially hot day. My friends grabbed "real" beers with names such as "Tiger" and "Tsingtao," which tasted like the same stuff grandpa gave me. Right next to the real guys was this brilliant green can with a bright yellow pineapple on it. With the percentage of alcohol, it was more of a "near beer" with pineapple flavoring.

It was my special occasion type of drink: Ping pong after work, grousing with friends about work, overly spicy noodles, etc. China's special occasion beverage of choice is *baijiu*. It's pretty much what Americans call white lightening or moonshine. Its clear liquid gives no clue to the volume of alcohol—ranging from twenty-eight to sixty-five percent—or the burning sensation it could cause. I'd seen friends who could down tequila cringe when sipping *baijiu*; I'd stayed away.

But this Spring Festival as Annabelle poured me a glass of Pepsi, Uncle was topping off a juice glass with the "good stuff." He was pretty insistent that I should share in the warm drink. Using Annabelle to translate, we came to a mutual understanding that I would *ganbei* the *important* toasts and Pepsi the others.

"To family!"

"*Ganbei!*" the cheer rose from the table as all of us drank the *baijiu*. I could feel the burn as soon as it hit the back of my throat and slowly scorched my esophagus en route to my stomach.

"*Ooo...uch.*"

Uncle smiled and laughed and then I found the air to join in as well.

The rest of the evening past with copious amounts of food, story, and drink.

In the middle of a random story, Uncle decided it was time for another toast. I deemed this toast not as important and washed it down with the American soda.

Suddenly, Uncle raised his glass to family once again. I reached for the soft drink.

"Family. It is important, yes?"

He had me. I swerved my hand for the clear liquor.

"*Ganbei!*"

"*Ganbei!*"

Whenever Uncle was unable to persuade me a subject was important enough for *baijui*, he always toasted family next to get me back.

As the stories and drink continued to flow, we also enjoyed the snacks Grandma had placed on the table. The little mandarin oranges were especially sweet, and it appeared Annabelle and I were in a race to see who could peel and eat them the fastest. After we downed the last ones, I switched to the leftover seeds for nibbling.

Grandma got up from the table, grabbed a handful of apples that no one had touched, and headed for Grandpa's table. I watched as she set down the apples and picked up all the mandarins and brought them to our table. Annabelle reached out for one, and I did the same. I must admit there was a brief moment of hesitation as a voice from my religious upbringing said, "You must not eat food offered on alters." I quickly rejected the Old Testament teaching for a newer one that states, "It's not what goes into a body that defiles it, but what comes out of it."

I enjoyed those oranges, and hoped Grandpa liked apples.

In the end, it was a fun evening for all of us. Uncle was able to get me to finish my glass of China's finest moonshine, and I was able to consume it over a couple hours and keep my wits about me.

It seemed only natural that Eileen would join us during the holiday break. She and her dad picked us up in the village, and we drove to the nearby city of Jiaozuo, boasting a population of approximately two million. The juxtaposition between Feng Zhuang and Jiaozuo was boggling to me. In only a few days, I'd adjusted to the quiet of village life and was then overwhelmed by the overbearing sounds of the city: Horns honking, construction work, people yelling.

Making the whole scene ironic was knowing Jiaozuo is considered the birthplace of Tai Chi, the ultra-slow, meditative martial art that calms the brain and tones the body. The road leading into the city features a roundabout that's flanked by statues in Tai Chi poses. The parks house similar statues and have a smattering of people practicing the martial art.

Bundled in our winter gear, we meandered around various parks. It was a typical Henan day, cold with grey skies. The sun did its best to beat through the pollution layers, but its warmth and yellow glow were unable to penetrate the hazy cloud cover.

Thankfully, I had two upbeat travel guides to keep me warm and happy by constant movement and witty banter.

The park eventually connected to the city zoo. I admit, as a kid, I loved going to the zoo or various animal parks to see the animals. As I got older and wiser to the way some facilities handled their animals, I wasn't as eager to visit. Topping it off, my first encounter with a traveling "zoo" in Henan was heartbreaking.

The previous year while walking through the park across from our university with friends, we heard an otherworldly sound.

"What the heck was that?" We all seemed to say in unison as we stopped in our tracks.

Tommy was the first to notice a massive temporary structure that had been erected in the middle of the park. The outer tarp was covered with pictures of lions, tigers, snakes, pandas, and other animals. It had the same aura as a circus sideshow tent: It looked entertaining but smelled of a scam. As we neared the enclosure, the sounds became louder, and it was apparent to all of us it was alternating roars and chuffs from a lion.

"You don't think they have a real lion in there, do you?" I asked.

Now that we were right outside the structure, it was easy to see its dimensions. The fifteen-foot-high walls made sure no one could sneak a free peek. The "zoo" was maybe the size of three average bedrooms and a living room. How could something as big as a lion be inside with other animals? I was imagining animal parks that let creatures roam about. I'd forgotten about little cages.

After much deliberation—and with the help of Tommy's amazing Mandarin skills—we determined it was a live lion and that we would go in and take a look. To this day, I'm sorry we did. The only consolation I have is hoping the money we paid went to feed the animals that were left. Inside the walls were numerous cages and aquariums. Some of the smaller cages were stacked on each other, while the lion and tiger, thankfully, had their own. The big cats were housed in cages that barely allowed them to stand and turn around. The tiger's massive paws pushed through the bars when it settled down on its side. The lion paced repeatedly as he voiced his displeasure and discomfort.

There were no special provisions made for the aquariums despite it being the middle of winter. The temperatures hovered around forty degrees on most days. The reptiles were dead or dying and management didn't see this as a problem. All of us felt uneasy and decided it was time to leave. As we passed by the cage with a red panda, a young Chinese couple by the cage picked up a stick and were using it to poke the animal. All of us but Tommy froze. He found a stick of his own and went after the couple.

"How do you like it?" he alternated between English and Mandarin.

The couple looked incredulous, and the manager got mad at us, but we were super proud of our teenage friend.

The Jiaozuo zoo, thankfully, was not like the cruel sideshow, but it was created in the vein of the 1960s American zoos with cramped cement enclosures. The animals that stuck out to me were the larger monkeys, who bounced around their cages like pinballs, and a giant eagle, who had maybe two feet of clearance when it stretched out its wings.

The zoo was not large, and, after walking a few minutes, we found ourselves in an amusement park. This is not to be confused with an American amusement park, like Magic Mountain. No, in China, amusement parks were for—as the name implies—amusement. It featured a large pond filled with giant blow-up, bubble-wrap looking cylinders that people paid to get in and walk like hamsters on the pond. There were small kiosks that sold snacks, bubbles, hats, sunglasses, and other trinkets.

Annabelle and Eileen bought bubbles and soon we were laughing as we tried to pop the floating soap spheres. I loved moments like these...simple things in life that reminded us that we were not so different from each other.

The following day, I returned to Xinzheng. Annabelle didn't ride the bus back with me. It's not because she trusted me to know where I was going; it's because a fellow teacher Michelle, who spoke fluent Mandarin, was on the same bus.

Michelle and I swapped stories on our experiences this time around. Between the ancient family village, the graveyard visit, and surviving the *baijiu*, it was clear I was the winner. We shared a taxi from the bus station and then went our separate ways at the teacher's apartment building.

Just like my return from Linda's, I jumped into a hot shower and let several days of living wash off me. I was exhausted as I fell onto my bed covered in numerous blankets. I couldn't wait for sleep to overtake me.

CHAPTER 21

I CAN'T QUIT THIS PLACE

A few months into my fifth year of teaching at Sias International University, I knew it would be my last. And I was at peace with it.

There were several determining factors, including the failing health of my grandparents, the increasing yearning of my parents for their only child to be in the same state, but most importantly for me, the nagging in my spirit that it was time to move on to the next phase of life. That original calling I felt to move to China, to push myself out of my comfort zone, to dive deeper into my faith, and to immerse myself in a new culture was quickly waning. The concern for my family made it easier not to renew my contract.

The downside was that I was still committed for the next eleven months. I had daily inner monologues about how to approach my final year.

Dude, just chill out. Coast to the end. You earned it.

What? No way! Go out on top, creating amazing lessons that students will talk about for years to come.

Ha, you're crazy. Why put in all the effort? Just use last year's lesson plans. They're good enough.

Come on, don't do something halfway. You're better than that.

In the first semester of my final year, the angel on my shoulder won most of the arguments. I had a great group of students in my classrooms and students-turned-friends to enjoy day trips and try new restaurants. The biggest win for the devil that semester was my refusal to join in any Culture Week activities. I didn't sing, dance, act, or write a script, but I did help to create small information boards for Europe and Australia.

Knowing it was my last year in China, I didn't return home for Christmas. I spent the first part of the winter break traveling with friends and fellow teachers Kerry and Laurie. We had twenty-four hours in Hong Kong—on my birthday—and then caught a plane to the Philippines. It was my second visit to the island nation. We stayed in Manila on the island of Luzon, then headed south to Boracay and Bohol where we were joined by Brandon—aka "B"—and Gabe. I went from being a third wheel to a fifth wheel, but both young couples were sweet and didn't seem too annoyed by this old American lady.

On Bohol, we traveled to see the chocolate hills, which are actually green during the winter, and then stopped at a roadside tarsier stand. Tarsiers are one of the smallest primates. They have ginormous eyes and skinny, stick-like fingers. They look like fat, wingless bats. While the primates were cute, the highlight of the trip—a Top Ten moment for my entire time overseas—was riding on top of the bus. Yes, on *top* of the bus. I often forgot that while I was on vacation, locals were actually working and a lot of them used public transportation. When the first bus stopped for us, I was certain they would tell us we'd have to wait for the next bus. Instead, I watched as Laurie and Gabe were pulled into the front door and disappeared into the mass of people inside. B, Kerry, and I were at the back door. B went in first, and I lost sight of him. The busman working the back "door"—there was no actual door on the steps—pulled me up on to the bottom step and Kerry joined me. The busman then straddled us, with his backside outside the door frame to make a door.

"Next stop, you go up," he told me.

"To the front of the bus?" I was curious how this would happen since I couldn't see any space inside.

"No. Up," he said and pointed to the sky.

Kerry and I exchanged glances and shrugs. Not too far down the road, the bus stopped again, and the busman scurried up the side ladder. He called down for Kerry and me to follow, and I heard Kerry call for B to come with us. Once on top of the yellow bus, I saw the busman and another man moving giant rice bags into a U-shape near the rear of the roof.

"You sit there."

They had made me a safety seat. I felt so safe and so free up there. The views were amazing. I could see green field after field and massive blooms of wildflowers. At the next stop, the guys called the girls up, and we had a little rooftop party. A teenage boy showed off his English for us and tried to teach us to count to ten in Tagalog. We all failed miserably, but enjoyed a good laugh at all of our expenses.

After a few more days in the islands, I headed back to mainland China to spend Chinese New Year with Annabelle and her family as my friends headed to Southeast Asia to continue their vacations. Trying to milk as much as I could out of my last year in China, following my *Bo'Ai* Spring Festival Trip, I invited myself/bribed my way into a Hong Kong trip with Shea, Aurora, Sarah, and Gwen. Despite leaving *The Davis Enterprise* newspaper in 2004, I maintained a relationship with the editorial crew and wrote occasional travel pieces. After contacting the media relations department, I secured five all-day passes to Hong Kong Disneyland for the crew and solidified my place in the vacation lineup.

Hong Kong is an amazing city. Instead of speaking Mandarin, Cantonese is the main language spoken there. Thankfully, English is spoken even more. After spending Spring Festival in a small village of less than a thousand people, mingling with the more than seven million inhabitants of HK was mind-numbing. We ate our way across the city, took double-decker buses to soft white beaches, and spent a day with a Mouse. Growing up in Southern California, I can't even remember how many times I've been to Disneyland in Anaheim. The Mouse House in Hong Kong had several of the same rides and felt very similar, except for the dried squid on a stick.

After a busy and full winter break, I didn't want to go back to work. The devil on my shoulder was winning more arguments. The one thing that kept my head in the game was graduation. Several of my favorite classes were going to snag diplomas in June, and I was so proud of them all. Those last few months, I took turns taking them out to lunch or dinner and trying to seal final memories.

The gremlin on my shoulder was aided by new rules governing the style of testing from the administration. A greater number of questions had to be subjective to show the student's reasoning. Normally, it's not a big deal, but subjective is much harder to grade than objective. My blood pressure rose as I thought of extra grading time. Adding to my frustration, once again, a senior class of Chinese Literature majors were assigned to my newspaper class. The cherry on top was they had already taken the class as sophomores, but the university wanted them to have another English-speaking teacher before they graduated.

One of the fifteen spoke passable English, but the others hadn't needed to use it for nearly two years. The class monitor and I tried to get them switched, but to no avail. I felt horrible for them. This was their final semester in college, it was supposed to be easy, and if not easy, at least fun.

I rewrote my lesson plans specifically for this class. I tweaked them to resemble the first year I taught the class, but with more of an emphasis on current events. Even with all of the revisions and grading on a very loose curve, some of the students barely kept up. I dreaded creating this final. With the new rules in place, I couldn't just make the whole exam easy multiple-choice questions. So, I kind of cheated for them. I was willing to give a large chunk of leeway to the local way of doing things, but I wouldn't let students be punished unjustly because of some crazy new rule.

The first half of our classes was spent on sharing news stories, reviewing and learning vocabulary, and reading. The second half was more reading and writing, but what they didn't know was that I designed these to be similar to their final exam. I wanted them to be as familiar and comfortable with the process as possible. As I created their final, I was extra clear on my wording and extra extreme on answer choices for multiple choice.

Which of the following is a news value? A. Porpoise B. Proximity C. Poster D. Pepper

However, their subjective was going to be tricky. So I gave them the only edge I could, I let them bring their paper dictionaries to the final. (No phone dictionaries, I wasn't that crazy.) On the day of the final, I flipped through their dictionaries to make sure there weren't any extra surprise "helps" tucked inside before I passed out their finals. Each class was allotted two hours to take a final. In my previous years, the longest anyone had taken on any final I created was an hour. When the hour marker hit and no one—not even the top student—was close to being done, my heart broke. Even my proctors, Gabe and Sarah, came up and mentioned that they hated me and this stupidly long test.

I glanced back and noticed one of the men in the class had his head cradled in his arm on the desk. I thought he was done and just waiting for a friend, which had happened in other classes. As I approached to check on him, I realized he was asleep (a first). I gently tapped the desk, and his groggy face lifted until our eyes met.

"Are you done?"

"No," he said with a sleepy rasp. "So many words, Teacher, so many words."

"I know, but you can do it. Just try. Write down as much as you remember."

"Okay. I will try."

At the ninety-minute mark, the top student turned in her paper. Fifteen minutes later, two more students. At the two hour mark, I had to take finals from several students. The young man was still shaking his head.

"So many words."

"I'm sorry."

"Worst day proctoring ever!" the duo said nearly in unison.

"I'm sorry."

I rushed home and graded the tests. Usually, I waited a bit, but I knew all of them would be wondering whether they'd be passing their class. As I marked the tests, I cursed the administration and its stupid new rule. With every red X, I loathed it for its decision to force these students to take this class in the final semester of their senior year. I graded the subjection sections with my righteous indignation on the rise. I knew what each student needed to pass. I knew that each student would pass. Those were some of the best text messages of my life.

Hi, this is Kim. You got a 70 on your final. Your final grade is a C.

Oh, Teacher, thank you so very much. I have been most worried. This is great news. Thank you.

There was another reason I wanted to get my grades done early. I had decided I wanted to leave early. For the past four years, I had missed Mother's and Father's days, and I had determined to be home this year for Father's Day, which fell on Sunday, June 19th. The university had planned to purchase flights home for Monday, June 20th. I asked for special permission to leave on Friday the 17th. With my request granted, I put myself into full going-home mode.

It is customary for teachers who are leaving to have massive "garage sales" where teachers returning in the fall can call dibs on furniture. I had an overstuffed, faux leather couch that was the envy of all who visited. In addition to furniture, I had sports equipment, books, magazines, and various knickknacks that I'd picked up from my travels. I announced in all my classes that I would have English reading material available for free on a first-come, first-serve basis. It was an ingenious way to see everyone one last time.

With my apartment empty and my suitcases full, I caught a taxi on one of the rainiest days I'd ever seen in Henan. I knew I was in for the ride of my life when I noticed all the streets were flooded. It wouldn't be so bad except Xinzheng has some of the deepest potholes I've ever had the pleasure of crashing into on a scooter. The taxi watched as cars ahead of us suddenly dipped down precariously when they hit potholes. Never out of options, the taxi driver turned the car on to the *sidewalk*. We drove two blocks on the sidewalk as pedestrians stepped into doorways to avoid the car. Once we were out of the city, the roads had puddles, but they could easily be navigated.

Aww, China, thanks for one crazy last ride.

The Zhengzhou airport was crowded but not crazy. My flight was on time when I checked in, but by the time I reached the gate, it was delayed. I didn't think too much of it until the ten minute delay turned into thirty minutes and then into "not sure." A thirty minute delay would still allow me to make my connection in Shanghai to San Francisco. A not-sure-how-many-minute delay was unnerving. The lady at the customer service desk assured me it would be fine.

Almost an hour later, the flight was finally up and on its way to Shanghai. The entire flight featured mild turbulence and major annoyance. By then, I was not the only person asking flight attendants about our landing time and connection gates. After the captain announced the flight was fifteen minutes out from Shanghai, the flight attendant told me to get up. I was confused and unsure, but the passenger next to me said in strong English, "She said, go up." (I was not getting on the roof of the plane.)

She also had the other passengers who had connections stand and signaled for us to move toward the front of the plane. Two things I know: One, you're not supposed to stand in an aisle during landing, and two, after 9/11, crews don't like people hanging out in the front of the plane. However, as we neared the pink curtain separating us from first class, a handful of people walked out of first class and passed us—they were not smiling. The flight attendant continued to motion and push us forward into first class and directed us to the closest open seat.

"This way you will get off first, and there are airline employees waiting to take you to the next gate."

I might have missed a few things she said as my body was melting into the overstuffed first-class seat. I'd never been seated in this section of a plane before—nor have I since—so I was going to soak up all fifteen minutes of it. As soon as the wheels hit the runway, the other faux-first-class people jumped up and into the aisle. It went against my inner safety monitor, but I joined them. We bolted down the gangway to the waiting employee, who seated us on carts and started to drive us toward our destination. I'd been in this Pudong International terminal many times, but this felt extra chaotic, even more than just being carted along at top speed.

The cart driver more slowed the cart than stopped it at the United Airlines terminal, and a couple of us more stumbled than stepped off it to try to catch our plane. There were a lot of people crowded around. I thought if all of us missed our planes, there's not going to be enough room. However, it turns out they were just there to protest something. I couldn't understand their demands, so I kept my head down and just made my way to the counter.

"I'm checking in."

"Sorry, we have no planes."

This seemed odd as I could see at least six massive United jets just on the other side of the three-story glass windows.

"Did my flight leave?"

"No planes leave."

"So, I can still get on my flight?"

"No, we have no planes."

I wasn't sure if this was the reason for the protest, but I was about to start one.

"There are planes right there. Are they going somewhere?"

"No. No planes."

With United firmly being no help at all, I found the check-in area for China Southern that I'd flown in from Zhengzhou to Shanghai.

"Hi, I was on the flight from Zhengzhou, and I was supposed to connect with United..."

"Oh, they don't have any flights. Their whole computer system is down."

Mystery solved.

"Do you have any flights to San Francisco?"

"No, sorry. No flights with the storm."

Without warning, I started to tear up. My already long day was getting longer. I don't even enjoy flying, but I really just wanted to be on a plane. The tears piled up on the ledge of my eyelids as I realized I had to call my parents and tell them not to drive to SFO because I wouldn't be on the plane.

"We could put you in a hotel if you need one," the lady said.

I mumbled my thanks as I walked away to find a quiet area to call home.

"Hello," at the sound of my mom's voice, the tears spilled over and I sobbed like a five-year-old. "Kim?...Kimberly, what's wrong?"

"There's not a flight out because of the storm. I can't come home."

My mother calmed me down and assured me that it would be all right. She told me to find the next flight I could and let them know when it would be arriving in the Bay Area. Armed with a task, I headed back to the United counter. Thankfully, there was a different lady.

"When is the next flight to San Francisco?"

"There is one scheduled for tomorrow morning, but we're not sure it will leave. Do you want to be on the standby line? You'd need to be here at five in the morning. No guarantee, you'll get on. There are lots of people waiting."

The overall weight of the problem came to bear on my heart. Hundreds of flights around the world had been canceled, which meant that tomorrow's flight with tomorrow's booked passengers was not even close to holding the number of people stranded in Shanghai.

"When is the next guaranteed seat to San Francisco?"

She punched away at her keyboard. "Monday."

I died inside. The whole idea of leaving on Friday was to be there for Father's Day on Sunday. If I believed the universe could laugh, it would be having a good chuckle at my expense right about then. I dreaded the idea of staying in the airport for several days, because typically airlines don't give you a hotel room for an act of God. I figured he was having a nice laugh as well. But then I remembered what the other agent said about booking me a room, so I booked a flight for Monday—the day the university had wanted to send me home, the irony was not lost on me.

I made my way back to the other counter and asked if I could still get lodging now that I had a ticket for Monday. The lady hooked me up with a voucher for the hotel. I joined the other passengers in the van for the fifteen minute ride to the hotel. The Pudong airport is on the edge of the city, not really near anything exciting to see. To top things off, I had exchanged the majority of my Chinese money back to dollars, which limited the places I could visit and use my greenbacks. So for the next two days for entertainment and meals, I caught the airport shuttle from the hotel to the airport, where'd I meander the shops and eat at Burger King. On Saturday and Sunday mornings when I got into the van, the driver would ask, "Today, you go home?"

I'd shake my head, *Bu*. Not today.

My time in the hotel was spent watching a little bit of ESPN, reading my Bible, and trying to figure out why I was stuck an additional three days in China. The Bible has a couple of big three-day events: Jonah in a whale, Jesus in a tomb. I figured three days in a nice hotel room was getting off easy. Wilderness-type experiences were never fun, especially, because I didn't particularly enjoy the lessons I was learning.

I spread out on the queen size bed. With my paltry five-foot wing span, I could lie in the middle and not touch any edge of the bed. I think about how ridiculous I must have looked rolling on the bed and how ridiculous some things are in China, and I laughed about both of them. I thought back to my first trip to China, when I spent three days in Beijing seeing all the fancy sights. My exit trip was three days in Shanghai seeing a lot of the airport.

Over the past five years, I'd learned enough Chinese to travel, bargain, and order my own meals. I had gone through military training and earned a Chinese name. I not only learned how to dance but also danced in front of a live audience of thousands and a TV audience of millions. I was treated like a rock star by locals and humbled by the generosity of the same people. I learned that I am God's favorite and did my best to walk in that grace. I laughed and wept intermittently on the hotel bed as memories flooded my mind. It was a chance to be quiet and be thankful for all I'd experienced in China.

On Monday, the van driver was a bit shocked when I got in extra early and I beat him to the punch.

"Today, I go home!"

"Yes, this is good."

He was probably starting to think, *this kid is never going to leave.*

The flight was so uneventful that we landed in SFO hours early. Usually, when I got off the plane and emerged out of customs, my parents would be waiting for me. Today, I walked through customs and there was no one to greet me. I watched as hundreds of other passengers embraced loved ones and friends. Then there was a lull before the next group came through, and I watched the scene unfold again. Even though I wasn't really into hugging, I felt left out. Finally, my parents arrived, and I got my hugs.

The drive home was the same as every other trip over the past five years. We exited the city, stopped at In-N-Out Burger, and continued inland to Sacramento. But this time, I knew there was something different. I would not be making a return trip in August. I would not be creating new lesson plans, giving lectures, or grading papers. This chapter of my life had officially ended.

For the next two months, I avoided Chinese food and did my best to settle back into life in Sacramento. The reverse culture shock was killing me. I didn't want to pay thirty-five RMB for lunch. Even though I was paying $5, my brain kept calculating how much it was in Chinese currency. The biggest purchase was a car. I sold my previous car before moving to China. Going five years without paying insurance, maintenance, or gas was amazingly freeing. China's transportation system spoiled me. While Sacramento has buses and a light rail system, it was not even close to being efficient enough to get me back and forth to my new job at my old newspaper. I bit the bullet and found a reliable, inexpensive car that got good gas mileage.

Life was starting to fall back into a familiar pattern, but a few things had changed that I couldn't go back on. I revisited my original home church, and it was great to see friends again, but it felt stuffy and overblown. It was too choreographed. Even after I moved to Davis to shorten my work commute and get out on my own, the churches I visited there left me feeling the same way. I didn't want a big building with set hours. I wanted, I needed a community of people, who would be there for me. It took me a while to figure out what that looked like for me, but I hobbled it together.

I was very particular in making reconnections. Before moving to China, I had a large number of people that I would call friends and an even greater quantity of people in the acquaintance circle of my Venn diagram. The same way I decluttered my closet, I cleaned out my friend list. It wasn't as if I called people and said, "I'm back from China, and you're off my list." It was a lot more organic than that. Some people naturally drifted away, and they never even attempted to contact me. There were some who I'd reconnect with and find out over lunch that we had grown in very different ways. They sensed it too, and we didn't hang out again after that. But thank God for the amazing, strong fellowships that were built before I moved, strengthened while I was away, and solidified upon my return. My new community is not all located in one apartment building. Sadly, some are not even in the same city, state, or country. But they are as close as a text or phone call. They build me up, they encourage me, they laugh and cry with me, they reflect the Father's love back to me, and, I hope they see his reflection in me, too.

When we do get together, it's as if we've never been apart. There are quick recaps of what everyone has been up to, and then, usually, a lot of food and laughter. My Mandarin skills have fallen off greatly—but still *good enough* to get a laugh from Chinese people I meet. I once again enjoy eating Chinese food in the States, even though I've only found a few places that taste authentic to Henan. My dancing skills are worse than my Chinese, but sometimes when the right song catches my ear, my toes start to tap off the beat, and I suddenly find myself moving to the music and enjoying the freedom of the dance.

ACKNOWLEDGEMENTS

I am blessed to have had so much help in so many areas of my life and publishing this memoir was no different. I want to thank W. Brand Publishing for taking a chance on an unpublished writer, and a special thanks to Marni Davidson for introducing me to JuLee Brand. Here's to the beginning of a beautiful friendship. Major thanks to Shea Nairn, Corri Lobbezoo, and Shannon Smith who were there at the very beginning, creating writing schedules, editing chapters, and kicking butt when necessary. Also special thanks to Emma Finley for proofing and encouraging sessions. Shout outs to my community of supporters, including Laura Jensen Walker, Michael Walker, David Lacy, Chris Saur, and David Weinshilboum. Your affirmation of my writing skills is always appreciated. Finally, *xièxiè* (thank you) to all my China buddies. I have shared some of our stories in the previous pages, but there are some individuals who must be recognized again (in alphabetical order to avoid being accused of favoritism): Aurora Aisenbrey, Joseph Aranas, Lindsay Aranas, Andrei Haq, Dianna Haq, Heather Husted, Jack Lin, Autumn Smith, Rebecca Strayer, and Kat Thompson. I have done my best to be authentic in my writing to honor the community that we built across the ocean. Thank you for being part of my life then, and for continuing to be part of my life now. I am better for knowing all of you.

Kim Orendor's online profiles will tell you she's a writer, but she sees herself more as a storyteller. She enjoys weaving a tale with the spoken and written word.

The bulk of her career has been spent watching and reporting on sporting events. She's clocked more than twenty years of experience between *The Sacramento Bee* and *The Davis Enterprise*. At *The Enterprise*, she won state and national writing awards and was the sports editor in charge of multiple state and national award-winning sections.

She even spent a summer writing greeting cards for African American Expressions.

Kim's career path took a dramatic turn in 2006 when she began a five-year teaching stint at Sias International University in China's Henan Province. The administration took advantage of her experience, and she taught newspaper and reading classes. She was later thrilled to get to teach American Culture Through Film where she learned the universal secrets behind storytelling.

Between the symbolism learned from films and the countless lecture hours, Kim was primed to become an Experience Expert (aka Tour Guide) for The Broad contemporary art museum in downtown Los Angeles. In her three years at the museum, she gave numerous public and private tours of the collection. Just as Kim had done with athletic contests, she broke down the artwork into understandable pieces, exploring the artists and materials. Kim's favorite tours ended with someone telling her they never thought they'd "get" modern art, but that her tour helped them enjoy the work.

Kim returned to the Sacramento area recently to become a caretaker for her father. She is once again working at *The Enterprise*, this time as an associate sports editor, designing pages and telling stories.

UNBOUND FEET